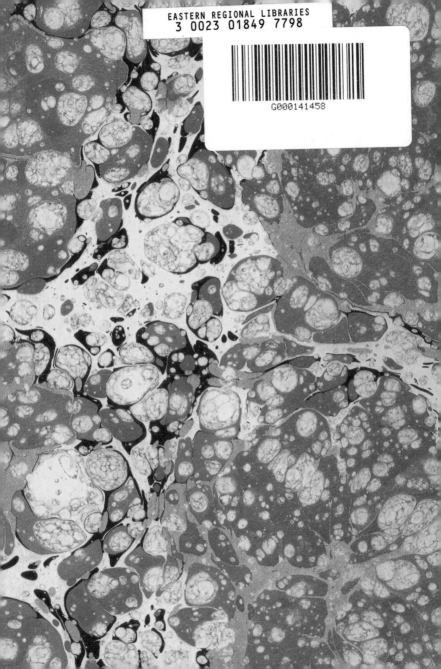

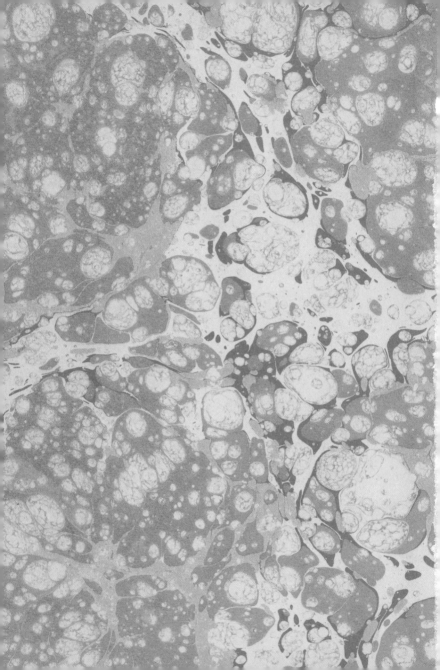

The Piazzas
of Florence

# The Piazzas of Florence

Lisa McGarry

PIER
9

# Contents

*For Ella*
Florence's piazzas hold so many moments of your childhood, from
that first gelato in your polka-dotted dress to all those memories
of blowing bubbles, flying paper aeroplanes and joining in on the
many celebrations.

# Preface

*I fell in love with the idea of Florence long before I came here. While studying architectural history at university, I found myself drawn into the stories of the multi-talented artists who gave Florence its churches and bridges, palaces and piazzas, and the graceful terracotta cupola that has served as a point of reference for nearly six centuries.*

*From the time I first walked through the city, when those secondhand memories came to life, I was enchanted. Experiencing a place on foot—following the curves of narrow streets that lead into broad piazzas; seeing beautiful art and architecture everywhere; smelling the scents of coffee, grilling meats and roasting vegetables destined for lunchtime tables; hearing the music of church bells filling the air—this was what I had always hoped for in a city.*

As a child I had wanted to be a writer. Since my ninth birthday, when I received the gift of a diary, recording my life in some form or another has been second nature. The entries from that first diary amuse me now—in a rather dull and matter-of-fact manner, they recall a routine of school and homework, sleep-overs and swim practice. Yet I am amazed at how these words have the power to recall that period of my life; between the mundane are small, but telling, details. After enthusiastically handwriting a one hundred and sixty-page girls' boarding school novel at the age of eleven, the dream of a writing career was somehow forgotten, although I did return to the pages of various diaries through the years.

When the time came to choose a major at university, attracted to a discipline where art merged with science, and intuition with logic, I chose architecture. But upon graduation, the depressed architecture market didn't offer many opportunities, so I found myself on a new path. I developed my oil painting and book-binding skills and ran a small business selling handmade items, finding that I preferred working with smaller, more hands-on projects. Treasure Boxes were my signature pieces, and as I decorated their surfaces with the papers collected on my travels or my own one-of-a-kind designs, I appreciated how they each possessed the fundamental elements of a building. Between the lid, the sides and the internal surfaces tucked within, the possibilities seemed endless. Creating limited-edition books eventually led me back to writing, and I began researching and publishing articles related to my new role as a mother. All along, I filled journals that I designed in my studio or picked up while travelling, using them to record my thoughts, develop creative ideas and explore the themes of architecture and design, cities and travel.

I always enjoyed how my travels offered a chance to breathe new life into my journal-keeping routine, and it was over the course of half a dozen visits to Florence that my approach towards recording these trips really evolved. Carving out time to note my impressions at the end of a busy day of seeing the sights had often been a challenge, but I discovered the value of creating a 'work of the moment'—how recording observations as they happen gives an appealing sense of immediacy that can't be substituted. So, while sitting on a bench in a piazza or on the steps in front of a church, surrounded by layers of history, architecture and art, I would make notes about the people, the activity, the buildings and the thoughts they all inspired.

Just as it was important to find time to record my experiences, I realised the advantage of designating a special place to put the

The Piazzas of Florence

memories before travelling to my next destination. Finding the 'perfect' travel journal proved impossible, so I started designing my own, adding a variety of papers, maps and other images, words and phrases in the native language and excerpts from books written by past travellers. This 'place' then became the foundation for the new layer I would create later.

Once I arrived at my destination, the fun of adding my own words, drawings, photographs and mementos to the journal would begin. Whichever technique I choose, I find it useful to think in terms of assembling a collection. I am especially attracted to collage, which is a natural extension of collecting: the process of arranging things in a way that looks pleasing—creating order through editing and shaping—is like a meditation for me. A pressed flower or leaf from a garden, a napkin or business card from a café, a beautifully designed admission ticket … each can become the starting point for a richly layered collage.

It's also helpful to keep a theme at the back of my mind. Colours are a favourite; I often watercolour the outside margins or whole pages of my journals with shades that capture my eye. In Florence, it's the subtle palette of whites and mellow yellows of the stucco walls; the many greens in the Tuscan landscape, ranging from yellow-green to cypress-green to olive tree-green to blue-green; the river's ever-changing browns and greens and blues. I then use these blocks of colour as backgrounds for notes, lists and quick sketches.

There are also endless themes to compare and contrast: the church façades, the rhythm of the day, the varied impressions of other travellers, the concerts held in churches and the events in the piazzas. I consider the differences and similarities I have noticed between the other places I have lived and visited, and wonder what it would be like to live in Florence's different neighbourhoods. At other times I focus on details, examining the numerous parts that make up a building or a piece of art: a remarkable number of elements combine to make Florence the rich whole that we see.

Even a simple list offers creative potential. I think of lists as a sort of written collage, and appreciate how memorable elements tend to emerge in the process of creating one; it's a simple way to capture a sense of the day. Making a list is also a great warm-up for more in-depth writing. Of course, answering the most basic of questions can also get your hand moving across the page: What time is it? What is the light like? The weather? What are the people around you doing? What do you hear? What do you smell? Whether at home or while visiting a new place, I like to begin my journal entries with a few notes on what's going on around me.

The extensive choice of journalling methods and techniques certainly adds a lot as I endeavour to record both the everyday and the special events of my life. Sometimes though, I find that just the act of picking up a soft lead pencil, a brush loaded with the perfect colour of paint, or a fine writing pen that feels good in my hand is all the inspiration I need to interpret my senses on the page.

While it's wonderful to return from a trip with a record of your memories, you don't have to stop there: the inspiration gathered from your travels can also provide a treasury for future creative projects. Notes, sketches, photographs and collages can be transformed into essays, reinterpreted as paintings and incorporated into three-dimensional work. My Florentine journals were the seeds that led to this book, which encompasses my original desire to write, an appreciation for architecture, my work as an artist, a love of the very form of a book ... and my dream of somehow making Florence a bigger part of my life. With much time, thought, discussion, experimentation—and the help of many people—the long-ago idea to create a book about my favourite city has become the one you now hold. As a wise woman told me along the journey, 'Anything is possible.' And my hope is that, whether you're reading the pages of this book or exploring the city yourself, you will find time to indulge in the many pleasures that Florence offers.

After that first visit, I returned to Florence each year. Finally, a four-month stay turned into a year, then two, then three. And although I have somewhat woken up from the dream of living in Florence—at least enough to realise that the city has its share of faults—every day I feel grateful that Florence *is* where I wake up each morning. When I hear the wheels of suitcases scraping across the bumpy streets, I feel excited for the discoveries their owners have ahead of them. I have stopped dreading the trip to the airport, which used to mean months away from Florence. Now I know I will be returning soon: Home.

# All roads lead to the piazza

At his villa on the hill of Bellosguardo—named for its beautiful view—Galileo could gaze not only at the heavens above, but also at the city of Florence nestled in the valley below. The small stone-quarrying town of Settignano, where Michelangelo lived during his early years, affords another glimpse of the sea of terracotta roofs. Many of the villas tucked into the hills surrounding Florence were built by the Medici and other important families; now their gardens are often open to the public, offering yet more perspectives of the city. Just outside the old walls, Piazzale Michelangelo's intimate balcony overlooks Florence, while a little higher up, the terrace in front of the church of San Miniato reveals an even broader view. Resting in the dip between two hills north-east of Florence, the Etruscan hilltop town of Fiesole presents the most sweeping panorama of all. It was at the Pensione Bencistà, just down the hill from Fiesole, that my first impressions of the Renaissance city began to take root.

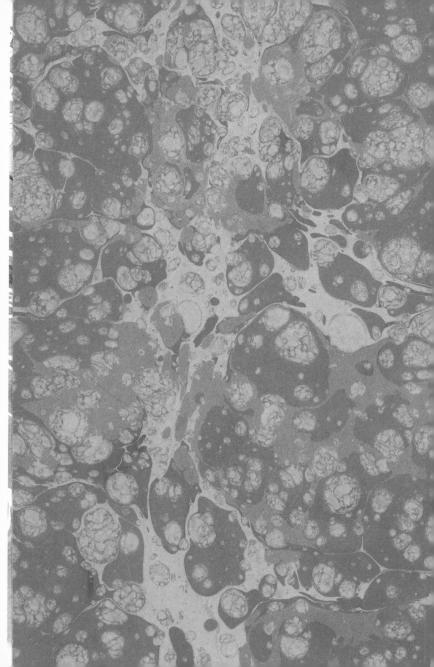

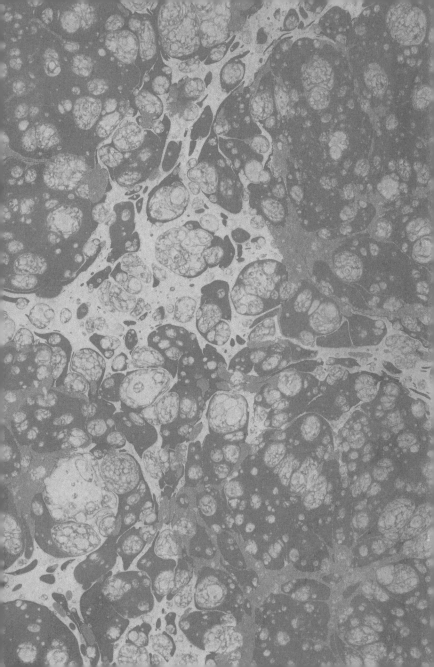

I'm sitting on the Bencistà's terrace, enjoying a post-dinner espresso while listening to the low voices of the other guests. Less than an hour ago we were all participants in a bustling three-course meal served in the high-ceilinged dining hall, but only odd comments can be heard now. We are drawn to the scene before us, which is strangely mesmerising considering there is no drama unfolding, no orchestra playing for us—only the lights of Florence floating below.

The Bencistà—where 'one stays well'—is a typical Italian villa, with the alterations of many generations co-existing as a harmonious whole. An original stone portion dates back to the fourteenth century, and the stucco walls of later additions are painted a buttery yellow that is cheerful even against overcast skies. A crenellated strawberry-ice-cream-pink structure lends a surprising note that only adds to the charm.

Since I first began staying here years ago, a number of modernisations have been introduced: the ancient playground in the front yard has disappeared, making room for a hammock and a ping-pong table; an elevator now simplifies getting luggage to one's room, which finally has its own private bathroom. But happily, the lemon trees in their huge weathered pots, the dappled shade of the olive trees, the pleasure of wandering from one terrace to another and the hospitality of the Simoni family remain unchanged.

The villa has a number of welcoming public spaces. There's a large drawing room with a piano, a parlour facing towards the city and a small sitting room that tends to attract guests looking for a cosy spot to read; bookcases overflow with volumes in several languages, left by decades of travellers. In the entry hall, business is conducted at a long refectory-style table, in impressive leather ledgers, and a bright sitting area next to a wall of glass

15

looks out onto an outdoor room with a ceiling of wisteria. Beyond, three levels of terraces overlooking the city invite guests to spend endless enjoyable hours relaxing and contemplating the view.

Staying at the Bencistà means joining its everyday rhythm— starting each morning with a leisurely breakfast, sitting on the terrace after the day's excursion, eating a delicious dinner in the dining hall, then enjoying a nightcap under the stars. This routine seems to naturally result in early slumber, especially as there are no televisions or radios to distract guests. I once had an illuminating conversation with an elderly British couple who had been coming here for over forty years. We were the only ones still up when the clock struck eleven, and the woman exclaimed in her proper British accent, 'Oh, we'd better be getting upstairs now!' As she stirred from her seat, she added, 'How things have changed—when we first started staying here, years ago, Signor Simoni was very strict about guests being in their rooms by ten o'clock. Everyone would be dressed in their finest, sitting around a beautiful contessa as she held court in this very room. At precisely ten, that was it— everyone off to bed!'

How lovely it is to be greeted first thing each morning by one of the dining- room staff: *'Caffé, thè, o cioccolata?'* By the time I gather my breakfast from the buffet, a steaming pot of very strong coffee, accompanied by another of hot milk, is waiting to bring me warmly into the day. In nice weather, breakfast is perfect on the terrace: a backdrop of Florence nestled at the foot of the Tuscan hills keeps us all company as we enjoy the warm rolls, baskets of fruit and fresh eggs laid out on the butter-yellow cloth.

After breakfast I take the bus into Florence. With the morning activities of the locals providing plenty of diversion while I look out the window, the twenty-minute ride into the centre passes quickly.

The route ends at the train station, where a hive of activity sets the stage for a day of crowds and sights, and the mirage I saw from the Bencistà's terrace comes to life.

The very composition of Florence fascinates me. There are the natural features—the fortuitously positioned river and surrounding hills—which have each played an important role in determining its shape. And then there are the built forms—bridges, walls, towers, palaces, churches and piazzas, with their varied shapes and sizes forming a rich and intricate texture. These urban characteristics were built in response to various political factors, both religious and civic, and together, they tell the story of Florence.

The hills to the north and south define the river valley much like a natural set of walls, creating a boundary around a bowl-like space that inherently limits growth. For this reason the city is very concentrated, although buildings do creep up the hillside to the north and south, and along the river towards the east and west. This theme of containment created by the hills is repeated in the weather of the valley, which holds close the biting chill of winter and transforms the city into an oven when it embraces the summer heat.

The river was an important factor in the founding of the first town. About 59 BC, the narrow crossing at this particular point inspired the Romans to settle just north of the Arno River. The new Florentia, meaning 'flourishing', was just down the hill from Fiesole, which the Romans had founded two centuries earlier. The Arno would also play a prominent role in shaping the city's future prospects, especially that of the cloth trade.

As Florentia grew more established, the town began to extend further south, but its growth was somewhat inhibited by the river, as well as the hillier topography that characterised the south side. The obstacle of crossing the river had initially been overcome with a ferry, and later by a bridge: communication then opened up between the areas on both sides of the river, and with towns to the north and south. In medieval times, the introduction of shops transformed the bridge into more than a link—it became a bustling marketplace as well. Florence's subsequent bridges also served as more than just a means of crossing the Arno: oratories, tiny houses and shops perched off their sides.

You can still trace the evolution of the city's shape on a map, beginning with the central Roman rectangle. While these first boundaries contracted and expanded depending on political circumstances, by the early twelfth century Florence had already started organising itself into a municipality, or *Comune*. Whereas the Romans had oriented Florentia on a north–south axis, the first communal walls in 1173 related to the angle of the Arno, a shift of about forty-five degrees. The walls then expanded in all directions, until finally they grew to include the river and the land to the other side; the later walls of 1284 assumed an irregular polygon shape. The combined effects of warring factions within the city, the terrible flood of 1333, and the plague in 1348 (known as the Black Death), shrank the population by at least half, so the thirteenth-century walls were the last.

In 1865, as the capital of a unified Italy (and no longer consumed by internal or external strife), Florence launched a comprehensive urban plan to make the city seem more impressive and accessible. After protecting the city for two millennia, the stone walls were dismantled and transformed into a series of *viali*, grand boulevards. Fortunately, long stretches of walls to the south of the river escaped this zealous demolition, and the city's old outline can still be seen in the course of the *viali* and the remaining gates that dot it at regular intervals. While Florence was always intrinsically different from the fortified hilltop towns—Siena, Lucca, San Gimignano, Cortona, Montepulciano and dozens of others—a big part of its identity and charm was lost when the walls disappeared.

Many of the private family towers have also disappeared, as rival families often took revenge on each other by demolishing them. What remains of these *torri* still serves as a reminder of the powerful and wealthy citizens who built them, and of the days when allied families were forced to unite in a city of civil unrest. Others survive only as considerably shortened versions of their once proud selves; the *Primo Popolo*, Florence's first organised government, had stipulated their height be reduced to allow the civic palace more impact. You can still find truncated versions of the old private towers as you walk through the historic centre, but the only ones emerging from the sea of roofs today belong to the churches and the major civic buildings: the original Palazzo del Popolo and its grander replacement, Palazzo Vecchio.

The church complexes that developed in the thirteenth century, especially those of the major churches at the heart of each quarter, have remained an important urban feature. For centuries, their prominence, position and function as indoor meeting places for both religious and civic purposes have given Florentines a neighbourhood focal point. The grand scale of these complexes, coupled with that of the enormous public and family *palazzi*, goes a long way towards balancing the chaotic concentration of buildings found within the patchwork of city blocks. And the cupola that crowns the Duomo, Florence's cathedral, is the most important physical feature of the skyline—it is visible throughout the city, as well as from the surrounding hillside.

But of all the city's diverse features, the piazzas are my favourite. While exploring Florence, the streets invariably lead to these public squares: whether they lie in front of major buildings, head up the junctions of riverside roads and bridges, or nestle discreetly off a quiet street, they have always been an important part of the citizens' lives. Numbering over one hundred, with their varied shapes, sizes and characters, Florence's piazzas create necessary pauses, allowing breathing space within the compact urban fabric.

As forums for a vibrant exchange of goods, ideas and energy, open public spaces have figured prominently in urban life for millennia: in ancient times, Athens had its Agora, Rome its Forum. Nowadays, whether it's called a plaza in Spain, a *plaçe* in France or a *praça* in Brazil, this is where both everyday and special events take place. It's interesting that the English word for piazza—square— conjures up a planned, rectangular space that can be static and sterile, when in fact the Italian piazzas rarely assume such a regular shape. Instead, they tend to emerge as irregular volumes from areas that are otherwise dense with buildings.

Italian cities are most alive in their piazzas; they are such a natural part of life here. Just as they have for the past seven hundred years, people continue to congregate in these spaces defined by buildings that accommodate the layers of passing centuries—it's such a pleasure to sip an espresso, catch the drips of a gelato, or savour the cuisine and wine in one of the piazzas while contemplating a visit to a museum or church. The streets lined with handsome buildings, museums filled with paintings and sculpture, tiny trattorias tucked into narrow streets … these are all important elements of the experience of visiting Florence. But the piazzas give the city a beautiful sense of structure, providing space to reflect on the past and observe the present as it unfolds.

Just as Florence's piazzas offer opportunities to catch my breath while I wander through the city, the Bencistà is the perfect spot to retreat after hours of people and history, heat and noise. Returning early to avoid commuter traffic allows time to look back on the day while enjoying the late afternoon warmth on the terrace. It strikes me that these beautiful stone walls that absorb the heat of summer are also holding the glow that arrives each autumn.

Guests are drawn to the many terraces to watch the sun glinting on the buildings until it takes its final plunge. Some people have a pot of tea and a book, others an *aperitivo* and a companion; many have brought their postcards. But the city has a compelling presence that draws everyone's attention towards it.

As I sip my tea I find myself agreeing with those who express their good fortune in finding this tranquil villa—and privately disagreeing with the couple who authoritatively claim that Florence can be 'seen' in four or five days. Glimpsed, perhaps, but not seen, at least not in a manner that implies a relationship of any depth. It's true that the city can be broken down into a manageable number of highlights, but so much lies between the Uffizi, the Duomo and the Boboli Garden.

After walking for hours on Florence's uneven stone streets, it's a treat to sit on the terrace as I sort through the things I've collected during the day's excursion. This afternoon I write about my visit to the church of Santa Croce, note the menu of a wonderful lunch at Osteria de' Benci, draw a row of cypress trees gracing the crest of a hill opposite me. Too soon, the sun dips behind the hills and the light fades: time to take my things up to the room and get ready for dinner.

The Bencistà is quiet now; only the geckos skitter along the walls. Outside, the sounds of late summer hum loudly, pleasantly. I wander down the corridor to the tiny balcony at the end of this wing and creak the door open. The air has cooled, and a soothing breeze enters the villa.

As I look down upon the city glittering in the distance, I think about why Florence engages me so. Perhaps it's because you can't help but come in contact with the city. Unlike other places I've lived, Florence is a town where it is practical to walk to the bakery for fresh bread each day, to a café for a cappuccino in the morning, to meet friends and tend to countless everyday errands.

Many people I know prefer the grandness of Rome or Paris or London. Others can't relate at all to the idea of living in a city; their ideal is a mountain retreat or seaside bungalow. I also know people who don't seem to mind where they live, as long as the schools are good, the commute to work quick, family is near—or not, as the case may be. Florence feels either too big or too small for many. But for me, Florence is like the porridge, the chair and the bed that were 'just right' for Goldilocks.

Each of us has favourite places that are defined by unique spatial experiences: for me, it's journeying via the escalator from the Mid-levels of Hong Kong down into Central; crossing the bridges in Paris, admiring the jewels of the Île de la Cité and the Île Saint-Louis that adorn the ribbon of the Seine; or traversing the width of Central Park to go from the West Side and the East Side in Manhattan. In Florence, it's how the bridges are part of every day, seeing the dynamic element of water carving its way through the densely paved town as I cross from one side to the other. It's being able to follow the cathedral's shape as I circle Piazza del Duomo, or finding instant warmth when I enter the south-facing Piazza Santo Spirito from a narrow street that the winter sun can't reach.

I enjoy being an everyday pedestrian, getting exercise without trying. There seems to be the right amount of visual stimulation and a certain degree of mental privacy as I walk through Florence's streets, allowing my thoughts to flow. Usually the slower pace of cycling makes it possible to notice many more details than can be seen from a car, but even a bike seems too fast to register everything here. I like the feeling of the stones under my feet as I walk over them, brushing against the rusticated buildings while negotiating the narrow footpaths, joining the bustle in the piazzas.

Florence's many piazzas have each come to represent different things for me. The vast stone Piazza Pitti reminds me of an urban beach, while the intimate Piazza Santo Spirito is more like a big outdoor family room. Ponte Vecchio's tiny piazza lies at the middle of the bridge that links us to the other side of town, offering a spot to watch the river flowing through the city. Piazza della Signoria, Florence's civic heart, is like a huge container—for people, for celebrations, for my thoughts.

Because of my first experience in Piazza Santa Maria Novella, I associate it with perceptions—how they are formed, how they can change. Piazza Santa Croce's large open space functions as a sort of communal front yard, and illustrates how space in urban environments is necessarily shared more. As the site of the Forum in Roman times, Piazza della Repubblica has a long tradition as a place of exchange, and nowadays invites people to sit in one of the many outdoor cafés, or browse in the plant market or the bookstore. The concentration of grand palaces and designer shops in the Piazza Santa Trìnita neighbourhood inspires ideas for transforming design into new ideas. Piazza San Lorenzo signifies the Medici, a family synonymous with three hundred years of Florence's history, while a visit to the convent at Piazza San Marco, another square associated with the Medici, inspires thoughts of solitude and retreat. When I need a fresh perspective, I go up to Piazzale Michelangelo to look down upon the acres of rooftops.

Piazza del Duomo is home to the cathedral's terracotta-tiled cupola, which towers above the rest of the city, serving as an essential orientation tool. As I wandered through Florence on my first visit, trying to get my bearings and knowing only that the river was south of the cathedral, I would often catch a glimpse of the striking dome—and a clue as to where I might be.

# Piazza del Duomo

Piazza del Duomo and the adjoining Piazza San Giovanni are very different from Florence's other major squares, which are usually spacious, open volumes with buildings sitting around them like spectators. Instead, as befits their importance in the city, the cathedral of Santa Maria del Fiore and the baptistery, or Battistero di San Giovanni, take centre stage in their respective piazzas. Although hints of the Duomo appear from countless points throughout the city, there are no grand spatial preparations like those provided for the cathedral of Saint Peter's in Rome: Florence's Duomo announces itself quite suddenly.

A number of differently shaped spaces flow around Piazza del Duomo. There's the area between the cathedral and baptistery, which is always full of people crowding in front of the baptistery's famous gilded doors or waiting in line to enter the Duomo. Others are just passing through, heading towards Piazza San Marco to the north, or south to the busy Via dei Calzaiuoli, which leads to Piazza della Signoria.

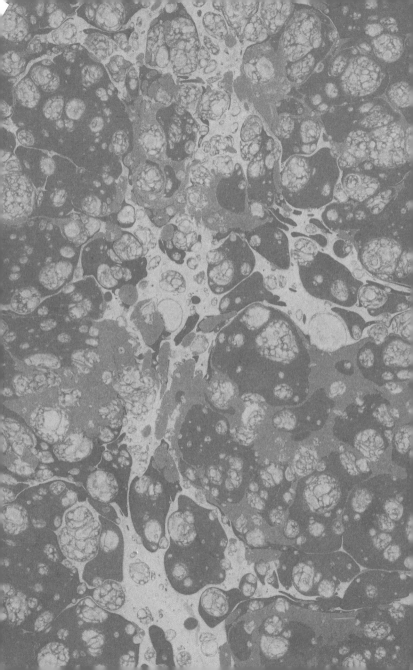

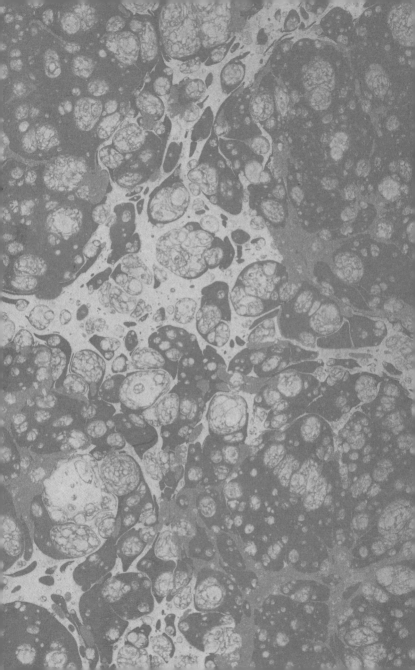

There's the area on the cathedral's north side, where the Duomo casts its shadow most of the day—a place to avoid in the winter if possible, but a refuge from the heat of summer. A couple of cafés sell cold refreshments, convenient for those waiting in line to climb to the top of the cupola. There are several shops, including a branch of Il Papiro, a popular Italian paper shop. Beyond this section of the piazza, along Via dei Servi, are more delights for lovers of paper goods: Scriptorium offers leather albums and journals, inks and pens, and Tassotti sells beautiful printed paper items of their own designs.

To the east, an area opens up near the cathedral's tribunes, with the ochre-coloured Museo dell'Opera del Duomo as the focal point—that is, if you don't count the mass of the cathedral itself; at this end is the cupola, which reaches a height of one hundred and fourteen metres. The piazza curves around the Duomo to the inviting south-facing part of Piazza del Duomo, where illegal vendors lay out their posters on the stone and arrange sunglasses on their ingenious cardboard 'tables', and caricaturists and watercolourists sit beside easels with worn samples of celebrity portraits on display. A number of shops face the Duomo's colourful marble side, including a favourite, Art Store. Run by Mandragora, a Florence-based publisher, it stocks a collection of books, typical Florentine stationery items, and one-of-a-kind jewellery, prints and pottery by local artists.

In the days of Florentia, this area was a residential zone, but the founding of the church of Santa Reparata some time between the sixth and seventh centuries established a long religious tradition on this site. Today Piazza del Duomo and Piazza San Giovanni cover nearly two hectares, but there was little open space to relieve the clutter that enveloped the baptistery and Santa Reparata until architect Arnolfo di Cambio's plans for a new cathedral were launched in 1294. The people of Florence declared they would have 'the most beautiful church in Christendom'. Since size was one of their measures of beauty, the thirty thousand citizens it was to hold admirably expressed their ambitions. In fact, the initial design blossomed impressively as the decades of its long construction period passed: the Duomo grew to a length of one hundred and fifty-three metres and a width of about thirty-eight metres.

In those times, churches played as much a civic role as a religious one, so the Duomo was really designed as an indoor extension of the piazza, and it served many of the same functions. The doors on both the north and south sides were kept hospitably open, allowing people to pass through freely and eliminating the long circumvention of the church's perimeter. This sociable and informal interaction between the city's most important building and its piazza perfectly suited the Florentine character: citizens could come to the cathedral to do business and socialise, as well as to attend mass.

More than a hundred years after building had begun, there was still no provision for executing the dome over what had become a much larger crossing at the end of the nave. A gaping hole allowed the elements to filter in decade after decade, until Filippo Brunelleschi presented his solution in a competition held in 1418. The architect offered an innovative and comprehensive answer to the dilemma: a double-shelled octagonal dome that would be self-supporting during its construction.

The judges were not so quick to embrace Brunelleschi's idea; they didn't believe the dome could be built without scaffolding or some form of support. The architect, convinced that no one else could solve the problem of the cupola, bided his time. Another meeting was called after Brunelleschi had privately consulted with the judges one at a time in an attempt to slowly gain their trust. Fearing someone else would try to steal his idea, Brunelleschi refused to show his model until he received the commission; instead, he made the unusual suggestion that the job should go to whomever could make an egg stand up on the table. Each of the architects tried, but none succeeded. When it was Brunelleschi's turn, he gently tapped the egg on the table and set it on its end. The others pointed out that they could easily have done the same, but Brunelleschi retorted that if they saw his model they could also build the cupola.

Eighteen years later, when Brunelleschi shared his plan to top off the cupola with a twenty-metre-high lantern, constructed of over four hundred and fifty tonnes of stone, citizens feared the additional weight and height of the structure would tempt fate. Lightning did strike the lantern repeatedly; on one occasion, pieces of marble fell into the piazza below. But the lantern plays a crucial role, providing enough downward thrust to keep the dome's sides from springing apart. And from an aesthetic point of view, it adds much to the overall impact of the cupola. Whenever I see the dome of the oversized Cappella dei Principi behind San Lorenzo church, the lantern never executed, it seems to be missing something.

A door from the cupola's lantern leads to a ladder that reaches up to Andrea Verrocchio's glimmering ball at the very top. Apparently twelve people (who aren't prone to claustrophobia) can squeeze into the sphere, which has a little viewing window. Most of us don't have the opportunity to access the ball, but anyone who doesn't mind paying an admission fee to walk up the four hundred and sixty-three steps can climb to the base of the lantern. Part way up the ascent, the corkscrew passage emerges onto an interior balcony overlooking the cathedral's main altar, where frescoed images of the Inferno in Giorgio Vasari's *Last Judgement* loom at horrifyingly close range. The remainder of the climb is between the dome's two shells, which makes it possible to see the construction details.

Brunelleschi's design is beautiful, efficient and timeless, and he seems to have thought of everything. He was an architect in the true spirit of the Renaissance, working as a designer, artist, psychologist, sociologist and urban planner. In his *Lives of the Artists*, Vasari describes how: 'Filippo had wineshops and eating places arranged in the cupola to save the long trip down at noon ... he supervised the making of the bricks, lifting them out of the ovens with his own hands. He examined the stones for flaws and hastily cut model shapes with his pocketknife in a turnip or in wood to direct the men ... In fact, he improved the practice of architecture and brought it to a perfection that it might not have otherwise attained among the Tuscans.'

The architect wasn't beyond using tricks when he felt the need. Vasari tells the story of how Brunelleschi was initially forced to share the commission for the cupola with Lorenzo Ghiberti, who had been Brunelleschi's rival since they had tied in the 1401 competition for the baptistery's bronze doors. Brunelleschi didn't want to share the commission, which is one reason why he left for Rome and devoted his time to the study of classical buildings. Ghiberti, however, did not actually understand how the cupola was to be built, and the fact that he was getting paid for a job he couldn't do angered Brunelleschi. The architect refused to come to the job site, feigning illness until Ghiberti proved that, indeed, he could not proceed without Brunelleschi's guidance.

As work continued on the cupola, Arnolfo's partially built façade remained unfinished and was finally dismantled in the 1580s. Over the centuries, it became the focus of several competitions and much debate. The Medici ruler at the time, Lorenzo il Magnifico, even submitted a design for the first competition—which naturally made it impossible to choose another one without insulting him. One of the most impressive exhibits at the Museo dell'Opera del Duomo is a multi-storey wall showcasing the results from the many competitions for the cathedral's façade. The drawings are large and rendered in minute detail—a testimony to the beauty of hand-drawn architectural renderings that preceded the crisp but lifeless computer-generated ones of our century. Although the actual designs may be somewhat static or rigid—the architects of that era were already imitating past styles with revival-this and neo-that—the drawings themselves are alive with the hands of those who drew them.

Not until three hundred years later did a neo-Gothic design by Emilio de Fabris finally complete the cathedral. As with all major city projects, it has been criticised—for being trivial, commonplace, uninteresting and too conservative—but it does harmonise with the bell tower, the baptistery and the original portion of the church's exterior, which all date back to several centuries earlier.

While each approach reveals a different slice of the Duomo, once I reach the piazza the colourful patterns and geometry are still an overwhelming surprise after the quieter tones of most of Florence's buildings. It never fails to impress me. I especially like the view seen through the slight gap between the façade and the bell tower; the vertical elements that make up the south side are seen at an oblique angle, their intricacy highlighted by the sun and the resulting shadows. And the door surrounds are exquisite. Border after border frames each door—every one of them completely different from the others. The façade is most lovely on an autumn day, just before the disappearing sun leaves the city in shadow. For a few moments the marble glows, defying the cold that it feels.

While the cupola inspires awe and the façade often provokes criticism, many people seem surprised, and even disappointed, by the Duomo's sparse interior. It's true that the cacophony of colours and patterns decorating the exterior only serves to emphasise the vast bareness of the vaulted interior, but I find its simplicity very beautiful. The frescoes inside the cupola, the colourful stained-glass windows around the dome's drum and the elaborately detailed sixteenth-century polychrome marble floor somewhat soften the austerity of the basilica, but little detracts from the power and purity of its architecture. The large nave almost serves as a corridor as its immense columns lead to the central altar under the dome, fulfilling the same preparatory role as the cortile in the piazza before Saint Peter's in Rome.

I think of how Constance Fenimore Woolson's key scene in her novella *A Florentine Experiment* takes place in the Duomo: after walking the perimeter of the basilica a few times, her characters were able to straighten out all the problems that had led to that point in the story. I enjoy this introduction of space—of architecture—into writing, and how the experience of circling the cathedral has been forever recorded in words by Woolson, especially since visitors can no longer follow the entire inner footprint of the building.

As I approach the central choir I remember the most shocking event to take place inside the Duomo—the Pazzi Conspiracy. In 1478, members of the Pazzi family devised a scheme to kill Lorenzo il Magnifico and his younger brother Giuliano—with Papal concession, no less. Their goal was to suppress the powerful rival banking family but, unfortunately for the Pazzis, the only professional assassin backed out at the last minute. When he discovered the venue of the assault had been changed from the villa in Fiesole to the Duomo, the man protested that committing murder under the eyes of God was too much for his conscience to bear. The holy setting did not deter the two priests who attacked Lorenzo, but they only managed to wound Lorenzo's neck before he escaped to the refuge of the north sacristy. Giuliano did not fare so well: when a friend of Lorenzo's looked down on the scene from Luca della Robbia's joyful choir, he saw Giuliano lying dead in a pool of blood.

All the conspirators were captured and dealt with in terms that would compose the worst of nightmares. Over seventy Pazzi supporters were killed: some men were stabbed and beaten to death, others quartered, their heads or other body parts then placed atop swords and paraded around Piazza della Signoria. Two conspirators (including the professional assassin) were beheaded in the Bargello's courtyard. Several were hung from the windows of Palazzo Vecchio or the Bargello, including Jacopo de' Pazzi, head of the Pazzi family at the time. He had managed to escape, but was found and brought back to Florence two days later, then tortured and stripped before being hung from a window. His punishment was thorough; legend says that after he was buried his body was dug up and dragged through the streets of Florence. His corpse was then thrown into the Arno, where a group of children apparently found him. They hung his body from a tree, beating him before tossing him back into the river. The Pazzi name was of course disgraced, and the remaining family members stripped of their property, papers and the right to hold office. Their name—incidentally, *pazzo* means 'crazy'—lives on in written accounts and art inspired by the event.

The Pazzi are also associated with the Duomo's most fantastic celebration of the year: the *Scoppio del Carro*, which translates as 'explosion of the cart', a centuries-old drama that takes place each Easter Sunday. Flints brought back from the Holy Sepulchre by a Pazzi ancestor in 1088 were traditionally used to light a candle that is carried by cart in a grand procession, beginning at the small church of Santi Apostoli near the river. The candle's flame was then used to light a mechanical dove at the Duomo's high altar (although rumour has it that nowadays a mere cigarette lighter does the job). Letting off sparks as it moves along its course, the dove follows a wire running down the nave to the cart of fireworks sitting outside the cathedral; once the dove has ignited the fireworks, it must return to the starting post. Sighs of relief then fill the city, as the dove's successful completion of the task guarantees a bountiful harvest for that year.

This Sunday morning feels like just another April day—sunny, lots of pedestrians on the streets, the cafés and shops open for business, with the usual Sunday exceptions. It's not until I have nearly reached Piazza del Duomo that I feel sure today really *is* Easter: the hordes of pedestrians have come to a halt, and a few blocks ahead, between the baptistery and the cathedral, *Il Brindellone*, the traditional cart containing the fireworks for the *Scoppio del Carro*, waits expectantly.

Once I enter the church, I wander among the crowds for a while, listening to the roar of thousands of people talking and the sweet voices of a children's choir piped over the speakers. 'It's almost as big as a soccer field,' I overhear a man say in Italian—the Italians always seem to have soccer on the mind.

I have never seen the church so packed. I finally find a spot by the altar, under the cupola. Centred before the raised altar is the column that supports one end of the wire, with the mechanical dove in the starting position. Helicopters are circling outside. There is a feeling of anticipation and excitement as I look around, taking in details that I have only read about before. Last year I was in the piazza and couldn't see much more than heads and shoulders. Even so, waiting in the closely packed crowd, hearing the spark of the dove upon its arrival and then the explosions of the cart—joined a few moments later by the joyful ringing of the bells—filled me with unexpected emotion. I am growing used to this fragmented way of witnessing celebrations here though—it's like assembling a collage or creating a mosaic of compiled memories over time.

This year I am able to see *who* rings those bells. I will always remember glancing over at the doorway to the south sacristy, where a priest stood in a perfectly placed shaft of sunlight, exuberantly pulling the bell rope once the dove had returned. In that moment it struck me how joyful Easter must be to a person who has devoted his life to the service of God. For many of us, it is a herald of spring, or an excuse for an extravagant feast, chocolate bunnies and brightly coloured eggs with surprises inside, but for Catholics Easter Sunday is the highlight of their religious calendar.

The explosions continue for a quarter of an hour. I hear the parade of Florentines in historic costume as it retreats from the piazza, and know that the police are stepping through the debris to remove the barricades now that the crowds have started to disperse.

While the party outside may be over, inside the real celebration is just beginning. It's exciting to be in the basilica, to find out what happens after the cart explodes—now it seems more like a prelude to the main event. Even though the *Scoppio del Carro* tradition continues mainly for the sake of the tourists, it thrills me to be part of this event that began nearly a millennium ago. How dramatic it must have been when the explosions used to take place at midnight, under a veil of darkness. Even without the cart, midnight is still a significant moment of the holiday. Just before twelve, having rested silent since midnight on Holy Thursday, bells from all around the city join in the joyous song, calling people to this first mass of Easter.

As the long mass proceeds, people continuously traverse the area in front of me, their shoes squeaking on the marble floor. I observe the many priests; there is one who nervously twitters around, emphatically gesturing, unconvinced that all is well; the bell-ringer, well chosen for his enthusiastic disposition; and the archbishop with his beatific smile. The cheerful priest escorts young women and men to the sacristy; later they emerge with baskets to collect the donations. All the while children are admitted to a sectioned-off path along the main altar, proudly holding Easter eggs in their arms, or carrying them in pretty baskets or fresh kitchen cloths. They will be presented for blessing in the sacristy, something I had read about but did not imagine still happened.

Throughout mass, a number of honoured guests are admitted within the octagonal-shaped altar: trumpeters, their almost fluorescent red medieval costumes slightly reminiscent of a Santa Clause outfit; members of the military; the handsome city council member who attends all the cultural events; a tiny hunchbacked woman whose iridescent shoes always catch my eye as she walks through my neighbourhood on the other side of the river. Finally, the holy men parade around the choir, wearing lace and floral brocades in shades of spring—green, pink, lilac and yellow. With a nod towards the thousands of international visitors who come to Florence to celebrate Easter in the Duomo, prayers and closing greetings are spoken in ten languages. And regardless of your faith, or lack of it, you can't argue with the message of peace and harmony that the archbishop encourages everyone to carry into the sunny day.

Standing to the right of the entrance façade and slightly apart from the Duomo is the bell tower, called the campanile. Its particularly graceful ascent makes it noteworthy, but this one is also unique for a Gothic bell tower. At its height, Gothic cathedral design integrated multiple bell towers, which sprang out of the church and tapered lightly towards the top—as if they were about to take flight, but were not sufficiently independent to do so. In contrast, the Duomo's bell tower sits foursquare and freestanding—a building in its own right. In Italy in general, and particularly in Florence, the Gothic aspirations for light and height were not realised to the same degree as they were in northern Europe. Instead, Florence was already making way for the Renaissance ideals that would emerge here—ideals founded on the more rational and logic-based classical thought and architecture.

Giotto di Bondone, who was in charge of the Duomo at the time, began building the campanile in 1334. In his *Lives*, Vasari offers a clue to Giotto's confidence in his abilities. Apparently, Pope Boniface VIII had sent a messenger all over Italy to collect designs from potential candidates for a commission at Saint Peter's. When the time came for Giotto to offer a sample, he picked up his brush, dipped it in red paint, and made a single perfect circle. The messenger assumed this was a joke, but Giotto assured him that the simple gesture would more than convey his talent; indeed, the Pope invited him to work at Saint Peter's.

I first heard this anecdote in my architectural history class. The professor, who always cried while giving the Michelangelo lecture (which filled the auditorium with legions of former students), would at this point draw an enormous perfect circle on the blackboard to illustrate the story about Giotto. I wonder how many circles he had to draw before he could accomplish this—and if anyone today would recognise this achievement as a sign of genius?

Giotto died three years after beginning the campanile, having only reached the band of hexagonal panels on the first level. The work was then passed to Andrea Pisano, who had also designed the first set of bronze doors for the baptistery. He executed a series of diamond-shaped panels above Giotto's panels, and completed the second storey. In 1359, Francesco Talenti finally finished the top three storeys while also overseeing the ongoing building of the Duomo.

Despite each architect modifying the design and leaving his own mark over a number of decades, the campanile comes across as a perfectly integrated companion for the Duomo. Not even John Ruskin, the English critic and author who disparaged much of Florence's art and architecture, could fault the 'shepherd's tower', as he called it (in reference to Giotto having tended sheep as a boy). Seen from the ground, Talenti's graceful Gothic windows contribute to the feeling of lightness, and as you ascend the bell tower they provide impressive vantage points from which to look upon the changing perspective of the city's rooftops.

Today is stormy—perhaps a strange choice of day to climb the campanile, but even more dramatic than usual. The rain blows through the large windows on each landing, drenching each of us who has decided to attempt the ascent.

After huffing and puffing up the four hundred and fourteen steps, I catch my breath before the view takes it away. Florence appears to have arranged itself into a living map: the rooftops lie below in ordered chaos, punctuated only by the domes and bell towers that help distinguish the various neighbourhoods. The rain has all but passed. An overcast sky hangs low, gathering the city and its surroundings under it like a cloak, making everything feel closer. There is a distinct contrast in texture and pattern between the softness of the hills and the geometry of the rooftops and streets. Blanketing the hills to the south are all shades of Tuscan foliage, and scattered among this verdant palette are blocks of terracotta, ochre, beige, pale rose and white tumbling randomly down the hills into a sea of roofs and walls.

The Piazzas of Florence

When I first visit a new place, I always appreciate being able to look down on it from a high-up vantage point, whether from a bell tower, a rooftop terrace, a skyscraper or a hilltop. In Florence, climbing to the top of the campanile or the cathedral's cupola has been an invaluable way to familiarise myself with the layout of the streets and landmarks.

One feature that stands out are the churches that lie throughout each of Florence's neighbourhoods. Many of these churches were first established by the mendicant orders in the thirteenth century, and they eventually grew into immense complexes that included chapels, convents, schools, hospitals and gardens. The most important of these religious complexes became the foci of their districts, and shared their names: Santa Maria Novella to the west, Santa Croce to the south-east, and Santo Spirito on the south side of the river, with the Duomo positioned at the heart of the central district of San Giovanni (named for the baptistery). These churches became an important part of Florence's physical and social landscape, especially once they were brought within the city walls when the final circuit was built towards the end of the thirteenth century. They also provide respite from the minute scale of the tightly knit residential fabric: this hierarchy of space is evident not only on a map, but also as one walks through the city.

A couple from northern California asks me to point out the church of Santa Croce, so I offer to walk them around the perimeter of the campanile's roof, showing them the landmarks in relationship to their map. From the bell tower's east side we find Santa Croce; its piazza has anchored the Santa Croce neighbourhood for over seven centuries. To the north of Santa Croce I point out a verdigris dome that proclaims its uniqueness as a synagogue in this city of Christian churches. In the distance, to the south of Santa Croce, Piazzale Michelangelo occupies a broad overlook with an impressive panorama of Florence. Higher up the hill is the bichrome Romanesque façade of the church of San Miniato.

At the campanile's south-eastern corner, the couple asks about a pair of towers. The crenellated one belongs to the Bargello, originally called the Palazzo del Popolo; it is now a national museum of sculpture and decorative arts. The pointed spire to its right rises from the Badia, a wealthy Benedictine abbey dating back to 978.

Due south of Piazza del Duomo is Piazza della Signoria, the city's present-day civic centre; Palazzo Vecchio, the city hall, dominates the square. Nearby, Orsanmichele fills an entire city block; niches filled with notable Renaissance statues line the exterior walls of this one-time granary and market that became a church.

I point beyond the river again to the enormous Palazzo Pitti, which lies at the top of Piazza Pitti. On the hillside behind the palace is the Boboli Garden, with the Forte di Belvedere slightly to its south-east. To the west of Palazzo Pitti is the terracotta dome and bell tower of the church of Santo Spirito, which is located in a lovely tree-lined piazza of the same name.

Moving to the south-western corner of the campanile, I find the huge arch that marks out Piazza della Repubblica, the site of the Forum in Roman times. Palazzo Strozzi consumes a block behind the piazza; it is one of many family *palazzi* in the neighbourhood around Piazza Santa Trìnita. To the south-west of Palazzo Strozzi, on the other side of the river, we see the shallow octagonal dome of Santa Maria del Carmine, and to its north-west, the pretty terracotta dome of the church of San Frediano in Cestello.

From the western side of the bell tower we find the long side of the church of Santa Maria Novella; its colourful marble façade is at an oblique angle, with a piazza extending to the south. Just beyond, the train tracks carve their way into the Stazione Santa Maria Novella. Closer to us is the large dome crowning the Cappella dei Principi, which rises behind the church of San Lorenzo in Piazza San Lorenzo. The blue-green metal roof beyond the church covers Mercato Centrale, an indoor food market.

On the north side, at approximately one o'clock, is the Baroque façade of San Marco church in Piazza San Marco, which is famous for artist Fra Angelico's frescoes; they decorate the adjacent monastery, which was home to the fanatical preacher Fra Savonarola towards the end of the fifteenth century. Santissima Annunziata is situated on a long block slightly to the south-east of San Marco; this church heads the first piazza to be designed with a conscious plan, beginning with a beautifully proportioned loggia by Brunelleschi. As we return to the east side of the bell tower, the graceful curves of the cupola dominate the cityscape. From up here you can really get a sense of just how many of Florence's important works are by Brunelleschi: the Renaissance interiors of Santo Spirito and San Lorenzo churches, the Pazzi Chapel and Second Cloister tucked into the Santa Croce complex, not to mention several palaces and the defining architectural element in Piazza Santissima Annunziata.

Standing at the top of the campanile, it's easy to see how the owners of private family towers felt powerful and important in their 'castles in the sky', as we, too, find pleasure in the different views visible from this height. This image has imprinted itself on my mind, leaving the gift of a mental map, and I always find a trip up here helps my visitors to find their way around. My sister—who repeatedly got lost whenever she borrowed my car in the United States—no longer shows up an hour after we expect her, as she regularly used to do.

The Battistero di San Giovanni was believed to be a Roman temple until well into the Renaissance. Its early history remains uncertain, but the original structure may date back as far as the fifth century. The foundations have alternately supported a church, a cathedral and a baptistery. The trademark facing of contrasting geometric marble was installed between the eleventh and thirteenth centuries, and became a source of inspiration for future Florentine buildings, including the Duomo. Arnolfo visually connected the new cathedral to the existing baptistery by using green and white horizontal stripes of marble to emphasise their structural elements, and the baptistery's octagonal floor plan is echoed in the Duomo's octagonal crossing and three tribunes.

Doors decorated with bronze panels adorn each of the baptistery's three entrances. Andrea Pisano designed and cast the first set, which originally faced the Duomo's main entrance. Ghiberti's 'Gate of Paradise' (so-called by Michelangelo) now occupies this prestigious position. While the doors certainly deserve the compliment of being dubbed the entrance to paradise, the name was especially appropriate because the area between an Italian cathedral and its baptistery was traditionally known as the paradiso. This spot where the two piazzas merge is always the busiest, as people stand before the baptistery and take a break on the steps in front of the Duomo.

Although the originals are now housed in the Museo dell'Opera del Duomo, the copies still show how each of Ghiberti's ten square panels gracefully expresses, through a combination of painterly and sculptural means, a sequence of events from the New Testament. Ghiberti also made the decorative panels for the doors that face north, where visitors normally enter; this first set of his shares the Gothic quatrefoil shape of Pisano's.

The eastern doors normally remain closed, but I once had the pleasure of walking through the Gate of Paradise to attend an evening choral concert in the baptistery. One of the reasons I so enjoy visiting these churches is for the chance to examine the endless details—here a ceiling of mosaics glitters overhead and patterned marbles decorate the walls and floor—but the music added a rich accompaniment to the experience. Seeing members of the choir appearing under the arches of the singing gallery that night was one of those magical moments I seem to find often in Florence.

A museum housed in a former Oblate convent near Piazza del Duomo offers another way of understanding Florence. The Museo Storico-Topografico—or Museo di Firenze Com'era, as it's often called—illustrates how the city 'used to be' in a series of drawings and models.

I like to study their copy of the famous *Pianta della Catena*, a wall-sized panorama showing the city walls intact and the same landmarks that are still visible from the top of the cathedral. Other maps and drawings depict the same piazzas we wander through today, and a large-scale model recreates the density and conveys the chaos of the medieval market that grew up on the site of the Roman Forum. In another room are reconstructions and archaeological findings dating back to the time of Florentia, as well as information on the area before the first official town was established. Few visitors seem to make it here (perhaps because some guidebooks aren't very impressed by the rather low-tech exhibits), but several hours can slip away as I decipher the clues to the old city displayed in these rooms. It seems the further back I look in Florence's history, the clearer the present becomes.

For centuries a forum hosting a multitude of daily interactions, today the city's religious centre remains a hub for many activities. The devout come to worship and the curious to gawk, as the Duomo and Battistero continue to serve in their religious capacities, and people of all ages and walks of life fill the piazza. Ever-present tourists bring the flavours and languages of many cultures, horses nibble from their nose bags while waiting for their next carriage-load of passengers, and artists luxuriously roll their r's as they cajole passers-by with: *'Prego, Bella,* I draw your portrait.'

I find these two piazzas that lie at the city's religious heart most fascinating because of the relationship between the buildings and their open space. There are many shapes a piazza can take, but the way in which Piazza del Duomo and Piazza San Giovanni completely encircle their most important buildings is unique. I feel a connection to this centre wherever I am; the Florentines' wish to never be away from their cupola too long makes perfect sense. I like the way the patchwork of endless details on the Duomo's façade remains bright, even under the grey days that fill the interior with gloom, how the thoughtful statues of Arnolfo and Brunelleschi quietly look upon the bustle as sirens from the Misericordia's ambulances call attention to local emergencies. And as the cheerful bells note the passing hours, I can hear them all the way across the river, from my home in Piazza Pitti.

# Piazza de' Pitti

'Let's go to Pitti Beach,' my daughter often suggests. There's no sign for Pitti Beach; this is our nickname for Piazza Pitti, where a hard, stark open space slopes up from a busy road to Palazzo Pitti. Ella and I have been coming to this square for years, first as visitors to the city, and then later as residents. Opposite the enormous palace, a door opens into the modest palazzo where my daughter and I live, and now Piazza Pitti serves as our starting point; from here we set off each day to my daughter's school, to take care of errands, to Florence's other piazzas.

The most direct route to Piazza Pitti from the north side of the river is via the oldest bridge, Ponte Vecchio. The road leading from it takes you into the area known as the Oltrarno or, as the locals say, consolidating di là d'arno into a single breath, Dilàddarno—beyond the Arno. This neighbourhood to the south of the river has a dual personality—that of an intimate quarter of artigiani who have been running their artisan workshops here for the last eight centuries, and also as the neighbourhood of the many wealthy families who built gracious palazzi in the fifteenth century. The grandest of theses palaces is Palazzo Pitti, which was home to Tuscany's grand dukes for three centuries, and then to Italy's first king, Vittorio Emanuele II, when Florence was the capital from 1865 to 1871.

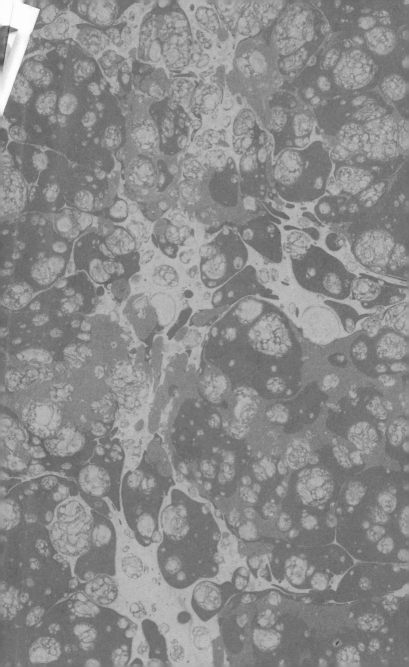

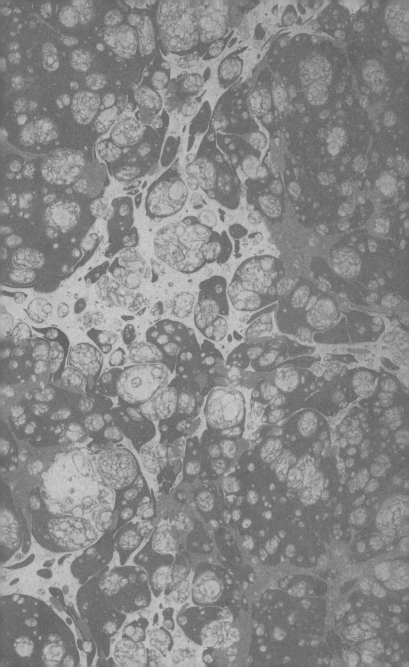

When the weather is pleasant, Piazza Pitti is always part of our Friday afternoon routine. After I pick up Ella from school, we shop for produce in the nearby Piazza Santo Spirito and buy pizza at the bakery. We then find a spot in the middle of Pitti Beach and sit on a sarong with our picnic, books and games, a ritual once recorded by a tourist who asked if she could take our photograph. In summer we breakfast in the morning shade, or enjoy a pot of tea in the late afternoon. Ella likes to skip and chase paper aeroplanes, while I enjoy the chance to let my mind wander.

The setting isn't very picturesque: cars and Vespas buzz down the one-way street, and the planters surrounding the sidewalk cafés provide the only greenery in sight. But to sit in the full sun, which warms up the stony environment—near to people, but not feeling crowded, as one does in much of Florence—is a good way to pass an hour. The space seems to invite everyone to spread out, oblivious to the traffic, as we simultaneously experience being part of both an impromptu audience and the show itself. Sandwiches and slices of pizza are set on paper-bag placemats, and guidebooks are put aside by tourists taking a break from historic details.

Two wings with loggias, called *rondò*, extend from the palace at right angles, defining and embracing the piazza. The ticket office for Palazzo Pitti's many museums and its garden is in the south wing, which also houses the Carriage Museum. Ducal carriages dating from the eighteenth century, including a gilt coach that sounds as if it belongs in a fairy tale, are part of the collection, but a long renovation has kept the carriages from public view for many years. The quieter north wing is only occasionally used for events, and makes a good spot for cartwheel practice and skipping contests.

The end wall of each *rondò* has a palatial storey-high niche. I still haven't discovered what they were originally intended for, but I sometimes think of designing a focal point to place within each one—perhaps a fountain, or something green and alive, to take the edge off all the stone of the piazza and *palazzo*.

There are many unfilled niches around Florence. I especially like the small cantina windows where wine used to be sold in the heyday of the *palazzi*; now all that remains of them are arched alcoves. Sometimes a shiny brass panel of doorbells or a mailbox is inserted within the space, but more often than not they have been cemented over, with only the stone surround as reminders of their original function. The city may be old, the Renaissance long past, but these empty niches seem to represent a possibility for future projects. Some people say that Florence lives in the shadow of its past, but creative minds will continue to breathe new life into empty spaces as long as they exist, and the new ideas juxtaposed over forms that have withstood the centuries tend to be all the richer.

At street level, along the palace's northern *rondò*, a line of umbrellas defines the alfresco studios of a number of artists, protecting them from the sun and the rain. Each artist has a different way of interpreting the city and the countryside from which it is carved. One woman paints loosely rendered human figures and Tuscany's signature red poppies; a character with flowing long white hair produces thickly layered cityscapes with his palette knife; another man highlights the geometry of the city's famous buildings. I think of this as 'Artists Row'; collectively their work seems more original than the others I have seen throughout the city.

Florence is full of contrasts. The piazzas are one example, in the way they offer breathing space among the dense city blocks. This is no truer than for Piazza Pitti, where the immensity of the square stands out against the intricate network of streets and buildings that lies before it.

The sun creates contrast too. The stone of both the *palazzo* and the piazza's paving is inert, enduring and never changing, and its monotony renders it virtually colourless. Yet the piazza comes to life once the sun comes around to cast its warmth on the people enjoying the beach-like atmosphere and the majestic backdrop of the palace. There's a play of light and shadow that isn't possible with slick modern materials, and the stone is so tactile that people run their hands along it, and sometimes attempt to climb the *palazzo*'s massive stone blocks. Dwarfed by the immensity of the palace, which somewhat resembles a quarry, people bring colour and energy to the piazza. Crimson banners advertise the latest exhibitions, adding another striking dash of colour against the neutral stone.

The hard, unforgiving landscape of Palazzo Pitti and its piazza softens into the pleasant refuge of the Boboli Garden behind it, providing yet another contrast. There's a wonderful diversity of spaces in this garden—symmetrical walks, meandering paths, shady allées, refreshing green lawns, fountains, grottoes—and many spots where you can catch glimpses of the city.

Looking at maps that date back to the garden's earlier days, I note the curves of some paths and the geometric layouts of others, which have remained essentially the same through the course of several centuries. This former quarry, which has supplied Florence with much of its stone, did not always have such a deliberately planned character. Only after Eleonora di Toledo acquired Palazzo Pitti in the mid-sixteenth century was the hillside of olive groves and orchards gradually transformed into the forty-five hectare garden that we can explore today. Successive designers took advantage of the sloped site as they combined the elements of water, plants and sculpture. They added structures throughout the garden, such as the Limonaia, where potted citrus trees were taken for protection in winter; nowadays, the space is used for exhibits. The Lorraine family had the Rococo Kaffeehaus folly built as a pleasant retreat for enjoying refreshments, and the café that is usually open there is due to reopen after being restored to its original shade of green.

Choosing my favourite part of the garden would be difficult. I like the idea of a Boboli Week—coming here every day for a week, exploring a different area each time. For a rewarding uphill walk, I choose the uppermost garden, which lies before the Casino del Cavaliere (now home to the Porcelain Museum). In late spring, a rambling rose shades a step that offers a perfect spot for observing the reactions of the other visitors as they are greeted by a fountain of mischievous monkeys, a low hedge maze showcasing peonies and roses, and views of the countryside all around. Ella and I have already planned out the olive grove on the hillside below, in case it should ever fall into our hands. Each tree and shady spot has a role: orange trees will grow near our breakfast terrace, providing oranges for freshly squeezed juice each morning; a tree house will nestle in a cluster of trees at the bottom of the hill; and we'll plant lemon trees near a shady patch, for making lemonade on hot summer afternoons.

Living across the street from the Boboli Garden helps me reconcile my preference for city living with the desire to give my daughter the green space she needs. Here we discover hidden rooms among the shrubbery, to which Ella brings order, adding domestic touches with leaves and sticks, berries and nuts. When we join friends for a picnic on one of the secluded lawns, the children can run freely, with no exhaust fumes or traffic to worry about. How the children would have delighted in the mazes that once existed on a sloping section of the garden.

We explore the southern end, where an arc of tall trees follows the curve of a large semicircular lawn dotted with wildflowers—perfect for decorating the miniature houses Ella builds for the fairies. We giggle when we see people, young and old alike, standing on empty pedestals and predictably imitating the poses of statues that lie throughout the Boboli Garden. Meanwhile, church bells from all around Florence fill the space at regular intervals, reminders of the city just the other side of this green respite.

As I emerge from the narrow Sdrucciolo de' Pitti at just the right moment late one afternoon, the glow of the stone on Palazzo Pitti surprises me with its warmth. The piazza is tranquil on this last Monday of the month, as neither the palace (always closed on Mondays) nor the garden (closed the first and last Monday of the month) are open. Many of the local shops and cafés choose this day for their weekly break too. Today's rain has washed the piazza clean: still glistening, it remains peaceful for now.

I turn the corner to return home. Our building is one of many with a *lapide*—a stone plaque—over the door, attesting to the presence of a famous resident at some point. Author and artist Carlo Levi lived here for sixteen months, beginning in August 1943; the building's owner at the time, Anna Maria Ichino, hid a number of anti-Fascists on the uppermost level of her home. Under a skylight concealed at street level, Levi continued his oil painting and finished the manuscript for *Christ Stopped at Eboli*, a book whose title baffles many readers. It describes a period when Levi was banished to the south of Italy because of his support of the Resistance, and he chose the title of the book to express how the villages in this area were so far south—so remote from 'civilisation'—that Christianity hadn't reached the inhabitants, who were pagan, almost witch-like, and considered themselves barely human.

Later in the twentieth century, each of the three residential levels of the eighteenth-century *palazzo* was eventually purchased by a different family. Ours is the only one that has been further split into two apartments; when the owner of the top floor gave his apartment to his son, it was in such bad shape that he had to sell part of it in order to pay for renovating the rest for his family. An architect bought it and worked wonders with what is now our home.

The first time I walked in the door, out of breath from climbing the fifty-five steps, I felt immediately at home. The floors are dark wood, which I'd always wished for, and the walls a golden yellow, almost identical to the colour I had painted our house in the United States. While the low ceilings in one half of the apartment have traditional wooden beams with terracotta tiles, the main rooms are several metres high.

The apartment's layout suits us perfectly, almost as if we'd had it custom designed. The studio is the best room: its window gets the most light and offers the largest amount of visible sky. An old-fashioned school desk that has been in my family as long as I can remember sits by the window, its fold-out seat stacked with piles of reading material. On the other side of the window is an armchair with another desk next to it, where I like to read and daydream. My easel, paints, canvases and palettes, and stacks of boxes of fabrics, papers and files are all crammed under stairs leading up to my sleeping loft; the steps themselves are always cluttered with books. At a long table in the middle of the room (my landlady's original dining table), I draw, paint with watercolours and create collages. Inspiration in the form of pictures, notes, sketches and artwork by my daughter cover the walls.

My landlady would be completely disoriented if she were to visit: I have removed doors from their hinges, replaced her wall art with my oil paintings, swapped her curtains for mine, put away some of her furniture behind enormous new wardrobes. In the few years we've been in this apartment, as in every place I have lived, the position of the furniture has changed dozens of times. I once read about a principle of Feng Shui that suggests moving twenty-seven things to bring new energy into a room (or other area of your life), and I have no doubt this works. The easiest way for me to get motivated to clean is to move the furniture—which would perhaps explain the constant flow of creative energy around here.

I marvel at the small details that make living here such a pleasure … the glimpse of Santo Spirito's bell tower and dome spires through my daughter's bedroom window, a small wall niche in the entry, the double-height ceiling in the studio that allows space for my sleeping loft, a window carved from an awkward space behind the kitchen sink. A narrow shelf accommodates a few plants, and there's a niched ledge just the right size for the blue hydrangea I buy each spring, which harmonises with the blue of the kitchen cabinets.

But the best part of the kitchen window is its view, which encompasses several blocks of rooftops before stretching all the way to the distant hills, with the sky filling the rest of the frame. A building taller than all the others interrupts the line of hills, allowing me to watch the reflected sunset on its enormous TV screen of a window. And of this I am sure: the many hours I spend in the kitchen are much more pleasant because of that little window.

I was somewhat disappointed when I saw that, despite a Piazza Pitti address, the main windows of our apartment faced not the piazza but the Sdrucciolo de' Pitti. A one-block street, whose name means 'sloped lane of the Pitti', it connects Piazza Pitti and Piazza Santo Spirito.

But since moving here I have grown content with this position: we have spent many hours watching the vibrant street life from the windows, and we can see a slice of Piazza Pitti, where a lot happens. Each November runners in the Florence Marathon fly past; the procession of the Magi begins here on Epiphany, marking the end of the Christmas holidays; sports cars, antique cars, bicycles and motorcycles frequently take this route on their parades and races; the Olympic torch was carried past on its way from Athens to Torino in 2006. We see many of these events twice: they head south through the piazza and then make a hairpin turn in Piazza San Felice to come north on Via Maggio, which we can see if we look right.

In 2006 a visit from the Queen of Denmark inspired a huge event in the piazza: there was music, a parade in historic costume and a flag-throwing performance as Her Majesty sat in her special chair at the top of the piazza. The sounds of an orchestra and thousands of merry-makers welcomed 2007, and we found we could see the stage far better from our window than from down on the sloped piazza. Even as I write, at midnight, the Corteo Storico della Repubblica Fiorentina and the Bandierai degli Uffizi have been performing at a private event held at Palazzo Pitti. This contingent of Florentines dressed in historic costume is often seen parading through the streets of Florence, accompanied by the beat of their drums as well as the traditional flag throwers; they show up in nearly every major piazza at some point during the course of the year.

From our windows over the *sdrucciolo* we see rooftop terraces, with laundry blowing in the breeze and candles lit for evening parties. Each March I watch the pigeons strutting around the roofs, checking out the 'real estate' before they build a nest under the eaves of the building opposite ours. Foxgloves grow out of crevices, making me think of local Welsh artist Rea Stavropoulos, who takes her inspiration from gardens—she talks about finding pleasure in even the slightest gestures of nature in this mostly paved city.

Each morning, the *sdrucciolo* announces seven o'clock: the metal shutters start to go up, the shopkeepers call out greetings and bicycle bells ring out. The personal touches that mark the territory in front of each shop are put out as the morning passes: plants are placed in front of many businesses and the handmade signs of others hung. The couple who own the tiny produce shop display their most tempting fruit at the entrance and unfold their metal bench with its faded cushions, where they will sit when business is slow. Goods from the *alimentari* (a tiny grocery store) jut onto the sidewalk.

Throughout the day, the familiar voices of the locals carry along the narrow street. At any given time, several of the shopkeepers are outside, chatting to each other and to the regulars who pass by several times each day, or enjoying the rays of the sun during the brief time it shines into this slice of the city each morning.

The *sdrucciolo* shares some of the characteristics of a piazza, even though there is no widening of the road here that typically signifies even the most basic of piazzas. It's the people who inhabit the space throughout the day that give it this flavour, a phenomenon that was especially noticeable when Italy was advancing in the 2006 World Cup. One weekday afternoon the shopkeepers plugged in a tiny TV on one side of the street so they could watch the game. It drew quite a crowd, who returned the favour with their business. The fans kept me informed of each goal as I worked in my studio upstairs; every so often I would go to the window to look down on the street event, which interested me more than the soccer game. At one point they put a piece of cardboard on top of the TV to help with the glare. It looked so third world, bringing back memories of cheering on Brazil in 1978: our television didn't have decent reception the entire five years we lived there, and I remember desperately trying to get a fuzzy picture of the World Cup games with a coat hanger.

Not every memory of the *sdrucciolo* is pleasant; sometimes I hear people arguing, and once I saw a woman screaming at a man as she ran down the street in tears. Another time a group of people formed a protective circle around an American girl who'd experienced an unpleasant trauma, and called the police for her. On these occasions heads pop out of windows all along the *sdrucciolo*—the Italian version of a Neighbourhood Watch. Little goes unnoticed.

A series of fortuitous communications along the little street gave one young woman a happy ending to her misfortune. At dusk one evening Ella and I were on our way to the *alimentari* when a young man clutching a purse ran past at top speed. A few seconds later a woman came rushing through the *sdrucciolo* as fast as her high heels could take her. I recognised the familiar look of panic and figured that her purse had been stolen (this had happened to me in Florence too, as a man tore past on his motorcycle). I yelled out *'Aspetta!'*—as if the thief would really wait—but I couldn't think what else to do. This drew Renzo out of his produce shop, demanding to know why I was yelling. As I explained the situation, a resident from the building next door came outside; Renzo commanded him to chase the purse-snatcher, advising a shortcut through the back streets. By the time we finished our errand at the *alimentari* a few minutes later, Renzo was excitedly explaining to a crowd that the thief had been caught and the woman had her purse back.

Each evening the plants are brought in, the shutters pulled down, and only bicycles and motorcycles line the *sdrucciolo*. There's such a contrast between open and closed; Florence's streets can appear so deserted at night or during the afternoon *pausa*, so it's always a surprise to walk by later and find them full of life. Along the *sdrucciolo*, there's almost always someone cycling or strolling by—a boisterous group of friends, students rushing to school, a tour guide proclaiming the history of the *palazzo* over a loudspeaker for all to hear. One night, just before midnight, I heard a roar outside, which became deafening when I opened the window: a musical event in the Boboli Garden had just finished and hundreds of people, animated after the concert, filled the entire length of the *sdrucciolo*. Within just a few minutes the street was silent and empty again.

Palazzo Pitti was not always quite so immense. Brunelleschi had offered the design to Cosimo il Vecchio, the head of the Medici family at the time, but he rejected it on the grounds that it was too grand. (The palace he commissioned instead, now called Palazzo Medici-Riccardi, can still be seen on Via Cavour, just north of the Duomo.) Instead, delighted at the thought of owning a palace even greater than that of the powerful rival family, Luca Pitti gave the commission to Brunelleschi (although the work didn't actually begin until 1457, well after Brunelleschi's death). A century later, the Medici family acquired the bankrupt Pitti property when Duke Cosimo I's wife, Eleonora di Toledo, purchased it as the new family home. Ironically, after a number of additions, the palace assumed a truly ostentatious size—its façade, more than two hundred metres wide, is three times wider than the one Cosimo il Vecchio had once found too imposing, plus there are the wings to the rear and the two *rondò* extending at the front.

The Medici grand dukes lived in Palazzo Pitti until their line died out, and then the Lorraine family moved in when they began their period of rule (with a brief interruption by Napoleon in the early nineteenth century). It became the residence of the royal family until Italy's capital was moved to Rome in 1871; the third king, Vittorio Emanuele III, gave the property to the State in 1919, and the building was finally opened to the public. We can thank the last heir of the Medici, Anna Maria Luisa, for the centuries of treasures that fill the *palazzo*—she left the entire legacy of her family's vast contributions to the city of Florence.

The grand ducal summer apartments on the ground level now house the Silver Museum, where a collection of silver, jewels, ivories and semi-precious stone objects are displayed in frescoed rooms. Half of the first floor is devoted to the Palatine Gallery, where a diverse collection of art has remained exactly as it was originally arranged—for aesthetic impact rather than in any chronological order. The Royal Apartments, where the king and queen's quarters are still preserved, fill the other half of the first floor.

The Gallery of Modern Art, on the top floor, is the museum I enjoy most. Many of Florence's important buildings and historical events feature in the works found in the sumptuously decorated rooms. The collection of paintings here dates from the eighteenth to the twentieth centuries, and includes that of the *Macchiaioli*. These artists were so named because of the spotty nature of their strokes (*macchia* means spot), and they give us a flavour for the peasants, the soldiers, the artists' families and the daily activities of the different classes in nineteenth-century Italy.

One of my favourite paintings in this gallery is Alfonso Hollaender's little oil, *Boboli*; I love the complementary shades of the glowing terracotta he used for the city in the background against the greens of the garden in the foreground, how he shows the city in its most favourable light. Once I was trying to sneak a photograph through the window next to *Boboli* and, instead of admonishing me (as the guards are often quick to do), the guard invited me to step onto the balcony. I found new views of the city's rooftops, a glimpse of our neighbour's enviable rooftop patio and the skylight under which Carlo Levi—whose portrait by Stefano Ussi I had discovered a few rooms earlier—wrote and painted during his months of hiding.

It's always hard to remember just how much area the Gallery of Modern Art covers. Although the ticket includes admission to the Costume Gallery in the adjacent Palazzina della Meridiana, I don't often have time to visit before the gallery closes just before two o'clock. The *palazzina* gets its name from a meridian line that was set into a wall of frescoes by Anton Domenico Gabbiani, which feature the themes of Science, Knowledge and Ignorance (in reference to Galileo's struggles with the Church). Now the cool Viennese decor serves as the backdrop for a collection of clothes and accessories from the eighteenth century onwards. Important Medici pieces are also on display, among them Eleonora di Toledo's burial gown and the pathetically tiny outfit of her fifteen-year-old son Don Garzia, who, along with his mother and brother, died of malaria.

Once I pass through Palazzo Pitti's large central doorway, I often have this sensation of almost getting lost behind it: there's no telling where I might end up or when I will come out again. Today Ella and I walk through Bartolomeo Ammannati's courtyard on our way to the garden. Its massive scale is in keeping with that of the rest of the *palazzo*, but I find it altogether too heavy; the grace and elegance I usually associate with its architect seem to be absent.

The courtyard must have provided a perfect setting for the most spectacular event to take place there: a staged naval battle held to celebrate Ferdinando I's marriage to Christine of Lorraine in 1589. The space was waterproofed using beams sealed with pitch, and then filled with water; the audience watched the show from the balconies overlooking the cortile. The later Medici were known for their extravagant celebrations—not to mention the public statues, columns and buildings they built all over the city and countryside. They brought several pieces from antiquity to Boboli, including an Egyptian obelisk dating back to about 1500 BC, a Roman basin from the Baths of Caracalla and countless statues from the ancient villas of Rome. The garden behind the Medici city home also boasted plenty of country amenities: the garden was kept stocked for hunting, a pond part way up the hill supplied fresh fish for the dining table and a menagerie of exotic animals was housed where the Limonaia was later built.

Nowadays, it's mainly just birds and fat cats creeping through the garden or lazing in the sun. As we walk up the garden's steep hill, we notice signs for Forte di Belvedere. Local friends have told us that the fort has finally reopened after restoration, so we leave the Boboli Garden through an exit near the Kaffeehaus and circle the tall ramparts, intrigued by a sculpture whose massing and prominent position brings to mind the prow of a ship. After ascending a steep drive at the fort's entrance, we reach the main level to find a multimedia exhibition, *Orizzonti: Belvedere dell'Arte*.

As with the Vasari Corridor, a private passage that linked Palazzo Pitti with their offices on the other side of the river, the Medici planned this fort with their convenience and safety in mind: they could reach it quickly through the garden, as visitors do now. Unlike the Fortezza da Basso, built earlier in the sixteenth century, the hilltop position allowed the Medici to keep an eye on the town itself—serving as a warning to the citizens, who had a history of revolt.

Francesco I built a 'small' villa-like structure, known as the Palazzetto, so that he would have a comfortable alternate home within the fort when necessary. As part of the exhibit, neon words follow the cornices around the Palazzetto's loggias, exploring the connection between art, society and culture. In the smaller garden at the back, a sundial composed of mirror shards and rods rests on a 'pond' of glass, reflecting an old sundial positioned on the wall of the building. The church of San Miniato, always serene, faces us from another hill.

From the city side of the fort, we can see Florence spread out below, crisply outlined in today's breeze. It's clear how the fort got its name: the word *belvedere* has its roots in *bel*, 'beautiful', and *vedere*, 'to view'. We look down over the exhibition's other installations— fruit (fresh?) spread out on tables of steel and stone, a forest of orderly poles sticking out of the ground, the 'ship's prow' sculpture that loomed overhead as we approached the fort earlier. We wander down and see that the fruit is indeed real, and marvel at their various combinations. I'm not sure what we're supposed to glean from this sculpture, but it's the juxtaposition of the colours that appeals to me: zucchini with eggplant, lemons scattered among pineapples and apples. As we walk through a forest of metal bamboo poles, searching for meaning, we hear the chirps of crickets and the croaks of frogs. Ella discovers a speaker in the ground—yet another medium. Next we approach the 'ship's prow', and a feeling of horror creeps over me as I realise that the sculpture is composed of parts that look like remnants from aeroplane crashes.

There are no signs naming these pieces of art, and no clues as to the artists' motives. I usually appreciate knowing what was on the artist's mind—it brings more meaning to the work, helping me to understand it better. But it has been interesting to see these unusual materials, combined for unknown reasons, under the Tuscan sky. The whole question of what constitutes art is a provocative one. This is light years away from what the Renaissance masters devoted their lives to, or what the Impressionists defined as art, but the varied pieces create a stimulating dialogue against the city's classic backdrop.

Once you've come this far, it seems a shame not to visit the newly opened Parco Bardini. The admission to the Boboli Garden also includes this dynamically designed green space, whose upper entrance is near the fort.

After following the path through the trees, Ella and I come to an intimate outdoor room. Part of the fun of our excursions is planning what to do with the great spaces we stumble into, and here I envision breakfast at the round stone table set in the middle—all that's needed to turn it into a perfect morning nook are pots of hot coffee and milk and a basket of warm pastries. Around the corner is a long narrow loggia overlooking the rest of the property, with a view of the city and hills beyond. It would make a wonderful summer living space. I imagine a number of rooms strung along its terracotta floor, marked out by furniture that invites summer reading, lounging and dreaming. There could be a painting studio at one end, a sitting area, a shaded eating space and wrought-iron beds surrounded by mosquito nets.

A lovely wisteria-covered alley just beyond the loggia is planted with several varieties of hydrangeas. Further down, a stepped garden has low stone ledges where one can pause and listen to the water flowing from fountains set into the wall; a small outdoor theatre carved from an intimate grassy lawn lies on the other side. As restoration work continues, many areas of the garden still have *accesso vietato* (no entry) signs, but the restored villa has recently opened as an exhibition space, and eventually the entire estate will be available to visitors.

You can exit onto Via Bardi at the bottom of Parco Bardini, or retrace your steps and return through the Boboli Garden. When I have time, I will go through the southern half of Boboli, enjoying the downhill walk towards the furthest corner near Porta Romana, one of the old city gates.

If you leave the garden via Porta Romana, you eventually come to a triangular widening in the road called Piazza San Felice, named for a church whose foundations date back to the eleventh century. We lived according to the schedule of its bells while renting an apartment in the nearby Via della Chiesa for six months, and still hear them through the windows in Piazza Pitti whenever the traffic doesn't drown them out. The poet Elizabeth Barrett Browning must have heard every ding and every dong from the Casa Guidi, where she and her family lived in the mid-nineteenth century; its windows and narrow balcony overlook the side of the church.

Another British writer who put Piazza San Felice on the map was Magdalen Nabb; she lived down the street from the piazza for many years, until she passed away in 2007. Among her work is a collection of mysteries set in this neighbourhood. I haven't read many mysteries since my Nancy Drew and Famous Five days, but I have picked up a couple of Nabb's for the fun of reading about the *quartiere*. She took her inspiration from the *carabinieri* at their station in Palazzo Pitti, and this gives her stories an appealing sense of place and character.

Nabb also wrote a series of children's books set in her native England, which my daughter discovered at the British Library in Florence. When the librarian heard how much Ella enjoyed the books, she suggested Ella write the author a letter, which she would then pass on next time Magdalen visited the library. When a response to Ella's thank you card arrived soon afterwards, we learnt not only that the author's home overlooked the Boboli Garden, but also that her son had attended Ella's primary school many years before.

A column placed in the centre of Piazza San Felice in 1572 is part of a design that finds its counterpoint in Piazza Santa Trìnita, which concludes an artery that begins here. As part of the ongoing Medici plan to enhance the urban decor of the city, Cosimo I had the column erected in commemoration of a victory at Marciano. The intended statue of *Peace* was never placed at the top of the column, and in 1838 Grand Duke Leopoldo II had the 'imperfect' monument removed to open up the road. It was returned (still statue-less) to the piazza in 1992, where it's now the centre point of a sort of roundabout.

Among the many businesses in the vicinity of Piazza San Felice we can shop at a *belle arti* shop for art supplies, a *mesticheria* for kitchenware, an *erborista* for natural beauty products, a wrought-iron home furnishings store and a coffee bar. The liveliest spot is La Mangiatoia, a *rosticceria-pizzeria* where you can either eat at the counter (and watch the pizzas being made) or in their dining room.

It's also a great place to pick up a takeaway roasted chicken and a few slices of apple cake.

As I continue the walk home to Piazza Pitti, I notice the plaques for other famous people who have connections with Florence. One is Francesco Mazzei, an architect who lived and died in the same house; he received much credit for his sensitive restoration of several of Florence's buildings in the nineteenth century. Paolo dal Pozzo Toscanelli, a fifteenth-century scientist and mathematician who assisted Brunelleschi with the cupola, lived at his family home just beyond the building with Carlo Levi's plaque. A plaque at number 22 remembers Fyodor Dostoevsky, who stayed here while he wrote *The Idiot*. On the corner of Piazza Pitti and Via de' Guicciardini is the family home of the Renaissance chronicler, Francesco Guicciardini.

Historians are still trying to work out just what gave Florence roots so strong that it could support the flowering of the Renaissance: some say there's something in the very soil and air. Whatever the reason, its residents are not the only ones to have benefited: countless visitors to Florence have used their Florentine experiences as the basis for writing, painting and other creative work. I only need to walk out my front door to inspire my creativity. Even the short daily walk to Piazza Santo Spirito along the *sdrucciolo*, where someone once put up a handwritten sign that read 'Florence's secret shopping street', is sheer inspiration. In one shop, clothing is designed and sewn on the premises by the owner; a workshop displays beautiful hand-coloured prints. There's a boutique featuring beautiful Tuscan linens, a vintage clothing and accessories shop with creative vignettes, a tightly packed antique shop, an upholstery workshop, a vaulted space where chandeliers sparkle—and my favourite, Beaded Lily. The owners, Lily Mordà and Tim James, work as a team: Lily creates unique pieces of jewellery as she runs the retail side, and Tim works magic with his bead lamp, producing a selection of beads both for the shop and a number of private customers. They have recently opened a studio just down the street on Via Toscanella, where Tim makes his beads and holds workshops for interested customers.

The summer solstice is nearly here, and already the summer we were eagerly awaiting a few months ago feels long. Through the open windows we hear the familiar beat of drums, so we poke our heads out to look for the Florentines dressed in their Renaissance costumes. Crowds of spectators are beginning to line up along the barricades that mark off the central area of the piazza, but there's no sign of the procession yet. 'Let's go down,' Ella says.

As we step outside the front door, we see a group of men and women, dressed in velvets and silks, and accompanied by drummers and flag throwers—a small cluster of colour in the vast square. From the far corner of the piazza another group is making its entrance. For the next half hour, one by one, the members of six Tuscan towns emerge onto the piazza, each with their distinct colours, drum beat and banner held proudly at the front. Finally, the familiar costumes of Florence's Corteo Storico file into the piazza, completing the top line of the square. Each group takes its turn pounding out a unique rhythm and showing off their flag throwers' skills, except the town whose representatives put on a horrifyingly realistic mock joust instead.

Being called down to Piazza Pitti for unexpected events like this, during an otherwise quiet evening at home, is another of the pleasures of living here. Just like our ritual of joining the crowds of sun-seekers for a picnic on the 'beach', it's simple entertainment.

I have really grown to appreciate this square's constancy, how it graciously accommodates everyone from the locals and the tourists to the Queen of Denmark. And there's something a little bit magical about coming home to the same piazza where Tuscany's grand dukes and Italy's king once lived.

# Piazza di Santo Spirito

*I look back on my earlier visits to Piazza Santo Spirito with a mixture of affection and nostalgia. The first time I found myself here, tracking down an archive of church façade drawings from a community project I had read about, I had no idea that it would become such a big part of my daily life. Or perhaps it is I who has become part of its life, its story? Each of us passing through the piazza, whether for a single afternoon or a lifetime of mornings, is contributing a new thread to its centuries-old tapestry.*

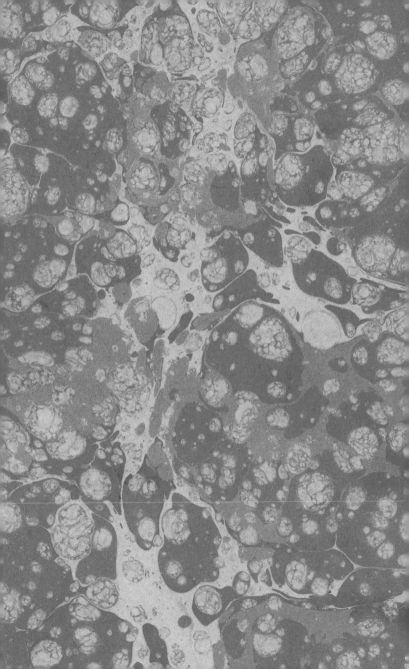

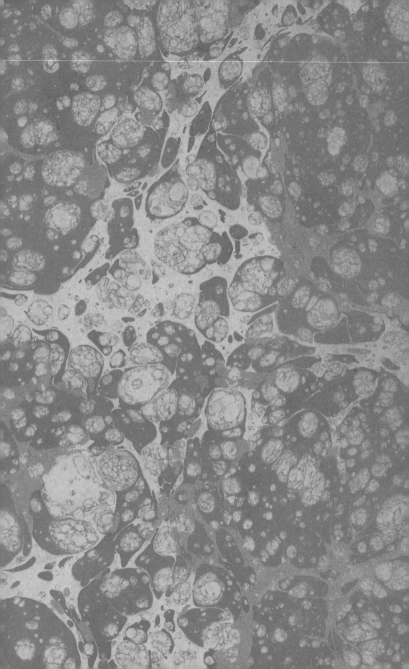

My first impression of the façade of Santo Spirito church was that it was unusual—'cartoonish' I wrote in my journal. I found it mildly exasperating that the church was always closed by the time I would finally make it to this side of the river, although sitting in the piazza waiting for the four o'clock bells to signal the reopening of the church was nothing but pleasurable. I could relax on a bench under the canopy of trees and observe the happenings in the square for a while.

By my third trip to Florence, not only had I become quite fond of this whimsical symbol of the *quartiere*, but it had also become the piazza where I felt most at home. Geographically, Santo Spirito became linked with the idea of home when we started renting apartments close to it for longer stays. While the front door of our present apartment opens onto Piazza Pitti, Santo Spirito is still very much our neighbourhood piazza, and the place where we tend to many of our needs. We come here to buy produce and school supplies, socks and pillowcases, cappuccino and gelato; we pass through on the walk to school and to the bakery. It's part of every day.

The combination of Piazza Santo Spirito's shade-giving trees, splashing fountain and sunny church steps seems to effortlessly put people at ease; in this most sociable of outdoor rooms there is always someone writing, reading, drawing or just looking around. Children gather here after school, clambering precariously around the ledge of the fountain, 'fishing' with sticks, or using it as home in their games of hide and seek. I watched Italy win the 2006 World Cup on a giant screen here, as I sat sweltering among the mass of humanity gathered on the stones that were still hot from the July day. It is where I bring my daughter to play with her hula-hoop, to blow bubbles, to eat an after-school snack. We sit near the fountain or in front of the church, alongside the locals, the tourists and the homeless residents who all share the space.

This is the heart of the Oltrarno. Only two blocks from the former ducal home in Piazza Pitti, this piazza reflects the other side of the Oltrarno's personality. An air of intimacy fills the square, unlike the large treeless piazzas that front the major churches of Florence's other *quartieri*, and the understated buildings surrounding the piazza complement the bold personality of the church's façade at the northern end. Offset and at a slight angle from one another, the piazza and church of Santo Spirito share a comfortable, informal relationship.

Visitors don't come here to see renowned art by the most famous of artists, or to witness the site of some gruesome drama in Florence's history; what draws them to Piazza Santo Spirito is less impressive but equally satisfying. At the focal point of this artisan neighbourhood, character abounds on a human scale, from the daily market that merges charm with necessity to the inviting patio tables spilling out of the many restaurants and cafés.

Nothing matches the atmosphere and bustle of Saturday mornings, when we have time to linger at a café, browse the *mercatino* and chat with friends who are also running errands in the piazza. Each weekday morning, the piazza has an offering of goods too: colourful household textiles usually brighten one or two stands, the sun reflects off the metal wares in another, and underwear, nightdresses and blouses flutter in the breeze of several. Produce-sellers display crates of vegetables for soup and pasta sauces, and fruit to replenish the neighbourhood's fruit bowls.

On the second Sunday of all but the hottest months, a flea market takes over the entire area, and the fountain almost disappears in the mélange of stalls, merchandise and people. Businesses that are normally closed on Sundays open to join the festive mood. Crowds browse the jewellery and trinkets, books and furniture, linens and beads, olives and dried fruit, and an entire row of plant-sellers brightens up the stretch near Via Sant'Agostino. I especially enjoy the stall featuring honey, sweets and beauty products made from essential oils, and the oils themselves, which are all sold directly by the family that produces them. You often need to use your elbows to reach the front, but will find the same attention and service that you would in a proper shop. It still amazes me how the Italian shopkeepers and employees don't seem to get flustered by long lines of customers; they simply serve each person as if he or she is the only one.

From another stand, a piece or two at a time, I am collecting antique cutlery to make up a one-of-a-kind set of dessert forks and soup spoons to use with my great-grandmother's china and my grandmother's Florentine table linens, bought decades ago near Ponte Vecchio and serendipitously returned to Florence when I moved here. I love this pursuit of bringing together items with long and varied histories, and which have been a part of countless meals at different tables through the generations.

The *Fierucolina*, a fair focusing on organic and hand-crafted products, fills the central area of the piazza every third Sunday, except in July and August. Each month features a different theme—a season, grains, sheep—although most of the same produce farmers, cheese-makers, bakers and artists show up each time. A lovely older couple cooks fresh *necci*, pancakes made of chestnut flour, and fills them with ricotta cheese if you wish. I visit a number of stands, assembling a sandwich of multigrain bread, fresh pecorino and greens, followed by a slice of wholegrain carrot cake and a bottle of cherry juice with the satisfying colour of red wine.

Once I ordered some beautiful custom-made cups for my morning coffee from one of the ceramic artists at the *Fierucolina*. The shape of the cup is worth considering; I decide which cup to use depending on what I am drinking. The handmade ones from the market are wide and shallow, bowl-shaped, with steep sides and sturdy handles, and the chocolatey plum and tinge of moss green with a whisper of white near the rim go beautifully with the milky coffee and layer of creamy foam on top of a cappuccino.

At Caffè Gilli in Piazza della Repubblica, *the* place to have a cappuccino in Florence, a conversation I overheard between the *barista* and a customer confirmed that a china cup, not a glass one—and certainly not plastic or paper—best complements the coffee. Disposable coffee cups are not used much in Italy; instead, little trays with tiny porcelain cups of *caffè* whiz in and out of shops and offices, supplied to the staff by the nearest café. A witty designer has recently marketed a clear glass version of the little plastic cups sometimes used for a takeaway espresso, complete with the usual moulded ridges in the design.

Just as I am wishing for another bottle of preserved tomatoes or a jar of honey, it's time for the next fair. Each month, as I recreate the treasure hunt for lunch among the stands, looking for my favourites and keeping an eye out for what's new, I am also continuing the search for a perfect slab of olive wood for chopping vegetables. Shopping is always more fun with a wish list.

The modest beginnings of this square and its church started with the settling of the Augustinians here in the middle of the thirteenth

century; their original church dates to 1260. Over the next century and a half, the complex expanded to include a hospital, hostels and refectories for the poor, and then schools and libraries once a circle of scholars began to gather here. To accommodate this burgeoning centre of activity, Filippo Brunelleschi was asked to design a new church in 1434, and to help pay for the new basilica, the monks gave up one of their daily meals in the *cenacolo* next door. Today this one-time refectory provides a home for the Fondazione Romana, a collection of sculpture assembled by art collector Salvatore Romano. This only remaining part of the original monastery is graced by a wall showing traces of a mid-thirteenth-century *Last Supper* and *Crucifixion* by Orcagna.

The piazza would have a very different character if Brunelleschi's original design had been followed back in the fifteenth century. He wanted to reverse the orientation of the earlier church so that the piazza would open onto the Arno, impressing those arriving in Florence via the river. What notoriety Santo Spirito would have enjoyed as a riverfront church, instead of being tucked into the Oltrarno. The wealthy residents whose homes were to be demolished to make way for the piazza naturally objected to the idea, so Brunelleschi retained the building's original south-facing position. Seeing the church façade soaking up the sun all day, the piazza in dappled sun, it's hard to imagine it otherwise now.

After Brunelleschi's death, several of his ideas for the basilica itself were also compromised. He had wanted the chapels to line the church without interruption, including along the front entrance wall. With the square module that forms the basis of his design, this would have meant four doors in place of the traditional three with which it was built. Brunelleschi had also planned for the exterior wall to express the curves of the chapels that line the church's interior, creating an undulating surface instead of a flat plane. Perhaps the slightly bowed sills under the windows are a small homage to the intended design.

Despite this compromise of his original design, Brunelleschi's genius is nonetheless present in the interior—in the harmony of its proportions and in the repetition of the architectural elements, which are delineated in grey *pietra serena* and strike a deliberate contrast with the white plaster walls. Only Giovanni Caccini's elaborate *baldacchino* of *pietre dure*, added in 1599—yet another case of Brunelleschi's (simpler) design being set aside—interrupts the flow of space in Santo Spirito. Standing under the dome, the canopied altar looks like a spaceship about to take off.

Spending some time in the serene interior, among what writer Mary McCarthy called its 'forest' of columns, is for me an unparalleled architectural experience. I sit on a pew near the back, as the space fills me with awe. Before leaving, as a small contribution to this institution that has anchored my favourite piazza through so many centuries, I buy a taper to light for anyone who might need extra thoughts of goodwill going their way. Who knows if these candles make a difference, but repeated positive outcomes—whether due to fate or faith—encourage me to continue the ritual.

I am sitting in Piazza Santo Spirito, watching the piazza's activity from one of the long stone benches. Tourists come and go, too restless to wait until the church reopens. Men and women rustle through today's news; groups of locals chatter away, their hands adding as much to the conversation as their words. The steps leading up to the church are filled with people enjoying the position in the full sun; gradually the piazza returns to life as the afternoon *pausa* draws to a close.

I consider Santo Spirito's façade, which is unusual compared to other Florentine church façades. A layer of pale yellow plaster conceals its stone and brick construction, while the other major churches—the Duomo, Santa Croce and Santa Maria Novella—are all faced with elaborate designs of green, white and rose marble. At the opposite end of the spectrum, many of the churches scattered around the city still present façades with courses of rough stone and brick, regardless of how detailed and finished their interiors are. San Lorenzo is a case in point: its interior is filled with an impressive collection of art and architecture, yet the façade remains exposed and unfinished.

It's not really surprising that the façades of these huge church projects do not correspond, or even hint at, the character of their interiors; the construction of each of these complexes spanned many generations of architects, artists, planners and patrons. Maybe this is one reason why they continue to inspire our admiration. The talent and energy of so many individuals combined to make rich structures that could not have been achieved with the build-it-quick-and-cheap mentality that is so prevalent today.

In her *Italian Days*, Barbara Grizzuti Harrison wrote how the façade's 'starkness would seem to invite the mischievousness of graffiti; it's a kind of miracle that this natural slate has not been scrawled upon, a miracle that stems from its incorruptible beauty.' I have often wondered what the solution to finishing Santo Spirito's façade should be; it's difficult to visualise an alternative when it has remained bare for so many centuries (save for the painted architectural details from the eighteenth century, which have long since been obscured). Better to follow a historic design or let it reflect our culture today? I feel that Santo Spirito's ideal form is *così*—like it is—continuing to be one of those topics that provokes an ongoing dialogue among the locals and visitors.

A project organised by artist Mario Mariotti in the early 1980s provided a chance for citizens to partake in this dialogue. Mariotti invited people from all walks of life to use the façade's outline as the basis for designs that were projected onto the church façade during summer nights filled with music, dancing, poetry and theatre. The results ranged from whimsical to clever and political, and art assumed its natural role—as part of the community, part of the present.

The walls at Ricchi, one of the cafés on the piazza, are covered with hundreds of these original façade drawings. My favourite takes advantage of the church's curvy outline and totally reinterprets the scale: a cat curled up in an armchair, effectively setting a huge upholstered chair in the family room of Piazza Santo Spirito. One drawing depicts a finger ringing a doorbell above a nameplate that reads 'Brunelleschi'; another superimposes a photograph of the church's interior, as if the façade had been peeled away. One artist wrote 'Homage to Filippo' in Italian, and drew the curved chapels as Brunelleschi had proposed. The winning entry was an image of a man sitting in a chair on a railroad track that leads into a tunnel—the church's circular window—and off to the side a scrawled comment states in Italian: 'Despite everything I will continue to plan my life'.

Another room leading from Ricchi's bar displays more original designs. There are several tables, where you sit without paying table prices, which usually range from two to four times as much as those if you stand at the bar, Italian style. (It's possible to avoid the potential surprise of *al tavolo* prices if you first pay and get the receipt at the *cassa*, go to the bar to order, wait for your refreshments and then take them to the table yourself. At many places, especially on the north side of the river, tables are only available with waiter service.) Besides excellent coffee and pastries, Ricchi offers *primi* and *secondi* for lunch, an impressive snack buffet at the bar during the *aperitivo* hour, and gelato and sandwiches all day, and their patio is a pleasant spot to watch the activity in the piazza during the warmer months. Next door, Ristorante Ricchi features fish for dinner.

We like to go to Ricchi for lunch; Ella's favourite part is decorating the outline of the church on the paper placemat. I appreciate how she can experience the link between the past and the present—a connection between architecture and art and community—as she too gets involved in the city's rich history of creativity. She notices how Santo Spirito's façade expresses itself in many forms throughout the neighbourhood: embroidered on the linen curtain of a trattoria, interpreted in the studios of artists, used by classmates as a point of reference in their projects.

Although I have yet to see a similar recreation of Mariotti's undertaking, various sponsors have reinstated the summer bar and entertainment tradition that has occupied the piazza from June to September for the past several years. The most magical of these evenings was when the Florence Dance Company danced their *Excalibur* program directly in front of the church. The show possessed a surreal quality, with the dancers' shadows flitting larger-than-life across the façade of the church and the scenery projected onto the church recalling the projections of the façade competition twenty-five years before.

Reminders of the show lingered for the rest of the summer, as the wooden platform remained in the piazza, weathering and warping in the sun and serving as a stage for uninhibited youngsters whenever the fancy took them. Twirling, jumping, stomping, their giggles echoed through the piazza.

With its live music, film screenings, wireless internet and bar, there's no doubt the summer program adds vitality to the area; it's a refreshing spot to spend those nights when the thick *palazzo* walls have absorbed their maximum amount of heat. On the down side, by summer's end the elegant fountain is often reduced to a rubbish bin, and I am beginning to understand why so many residents are against the invasion of their 'front yard'. From time to time notices show up, begging residents and visitors to respect the fountain as a part of the city's heritage, but the cumulative effects of laziness, indifference and inebriation inevitably manifest themselves again each year.

23 September. I just spotted the first *mapo* of the season in Piazza Santo Spirito. Marcello knew halving one to display its yellowy-orange goodness would tempt more customers. The flavour of this fruit that is a cross between a *mandarino*, mandarin, and a *pompelmo*, grapefruit, more sour than sweet, tastes like healthiness itself—almost akin to eating a lemon. Maybe resuming our kilo-a-week habit will stave off the back-to-school cold that's already doing the rounds.

Iliana and Marcello own the most abundant *frutta e verdura* on the piazza, stocking more than the farmers can, since they essentially serve as a middleman. They show the same pride in their goods, though, and won't take what a supplier offers if it doesn't meet their standards. They refuse to have numbers for the customers and seem to enjoy the chaos and the small disputes over who should be served next.

Marcello is the grandfather of the family, but exhibits the enthusiasm of a young boy as he rushes to refill and consolidate the display crates. 'Smell these cherry tomatoes! Taste these grapes, have a fig!' he cries as he flies around. Marcello and Iliana's son and daughter-in-law work there too, and their grandsons are often seen shelling beans or running around the piazza.

The Piazzas of Florence

All year long, a serene woman called Rosa sets up her table opposite the church. She has an umbrella to shade her from the heat and the rain, and during the coldest days of winter a small fire burns in a tin can. Behind Rosa sits a lovely backdrop of buckets filled with whichever flowers happen to be blooming in her garden. Before her is a variety of homegrown fruits and vegetables that range from gnarled to beautiful, although always incredible—green beans that grow longer than spaghetti noodles, and the small dusky green *justine* plums that taste as sweet as sugar. The common denominator: everything is flavourful and fresh (to the point that I once found a crispy caterpillar lying alongside my sautéed green beans). Rosa invites sampling, throws in a few sprigs of herbs to complement my choices, shares recipes and helps me in my quest to continue building my Italian vocabulary. It's a shopping experience that leaves me smiling as I leave the piazza to the sound of Santo Spirito tolling the quarter-to-nine bells, my favourites of the day.

The outdoor market here brings to mind the period my family lived in a small city in Brazil, and how each day of the week a market would appear in a different *praça* (essentially a piazza, only they were generally graced by more of a park-like setting than we see in Florence). In contrast to those markets and the ones in Italy, in my old hometown in southern California, somehow a grocery store could provide anything I desired at any time of year. Without the weekly presence of a nearby farmers' market, we could have missed the concept of seasonality altogether. Unfortunately it wasn't on my usual routes, and not close enough to walk to, so I didn't go to the market regularly; it was more of an event, something special to do once in a while. For this reason, I am still thrilled by the novelty of a two-block walk leading me to the best produce of the season six mornings a week.

We can buy just about everything we need in Piazza Santo Spirito. Racks of seeds and containers of baskets spill out of the tiny Civaie Morganti, while its interior is lined with grains, legumes, spices, woven goods and wooden trays and utensils. This is where I buy popcorn for our weekly movie night—and try to explain to the owner why I would want to grind granulated salt, my favourite garnish. (I didn't think the moist Sicilian sea salt would work very well in my grinder, so my solution has been to let the salt air before filling it.) Another time we stopped by for *grani di pepe nero*, black peppercorns, and the owner and my daughter both attempted to teach me the nuances of pronouncing the *e*'s of *pepe*. 'How do you say it?' Ella quizzes me whenever we walk past Civaie Morganti.

For meat we go to Valeria's *polleria*. Although *polleria* means poultry, Valeria sells a variety of other meats so we always find what we're looking for. I don't cook meat very often, so I appreciate that I can tell Valeria what I'm making and she knows just what to offer, or I can choose a cut and she'll tell me how to prepare it as she wields her butcher knife and takes care of the unpleasant stuff. Everything I've cooked from Valeria's shop has been good: chicken breasts flavoured with the rinds and juice of lemons and oranges; pork roast simmered in balsamic vinegar, garlic and herbs on the stove top for hours; *tagliata di manzo*, beef seared quickly in a cast-iron griddle, then sliced and served over a bed of rocket.

I have always wanted to live within walking distance of a bakery, so having one around the corner from the piazza is a wish come true. Cases are filled with long rectangular trays of colourfully topped pizza and a variety of biscuits, pastries, tortes and cakes. Just like the produce stands at the market, the offerings at Il Fornaio Galli also change as the months pass.

Schiacciata all'uva, a kind of focaccia—schiacciata means squished—shows up at the end of summer, when the small, almost black grapes are ripe, and castagnaccio, a dense and not very sweet 'cake' that tastes strange to my foreign palate, appears as soon as the chestnuts start falling from the trees. Christmas has its light and airy panettone, a tall, sweet bread with dried fruits, which I like to toast in the oven. Cenci, strips of dough lightly fried and dusted with powdered sugar, show up during Carnevale, the period before Lent, and are joined by little balls of fried dough filled with rice or custard, called frittelle, to celebrate the feast day of San Giuseppe (Saint Joseph) on 19 March. During Lent the Carnevale goodies are slowly replaced with quaresimali, simple chocolate biscuits in the shapes of letters; they were once the only sweets allowed during Lent. The colombina di Pasqua marks the arrival of Easter. Similar to the panettone but not as puffed up, with a delicious topping of sugar granules, its shape represents a dove.

Trays of schiacciata drizzled with olive oil and salt are baked all day long—a perfect anytime snack. My daughter prefers the schiacciata morbida, the softer, airier kind, while I like the Romana, which is denser and chewier. And then there's the bread: an entire wall features baskets with an assortment of loaves. The texture and crust of pane toscano cotto a legna, Tuscan bread baked in a wood-fired oven, is amazing once you grow used to its lack of salt. Another favourite of mine is lo sportivo, a 'sporty' multigrain bread with seeds, nuts and dried fruits, baked in sets of six knobs.

The bakery also stocks pasta, jam and wine, as well as various dairy products, which eliminates the need to go to the latteria for milk. I still remember the time I covered several blocks searching for milk for my then toddler daughter; I finally decided to overcome my reluctance to speak the language and asked a shopkeeper where one could buy *latte*. 'You need to go to the *latteria*, of course.' Fortunately, the segregation of products seems less strict on this side of the river—the numerous small *alimentari* sell a variety of items— but the bakery is still the only place in my neighbourhood where I can buy eggs on a Sunday in case we want to do some baking after having finished all the eggs at breakfast.

Gathering our daily bread—and produce, dairy and meat—has become a big part of our lives since we started living in Florence. But the process not only contributes to the obvious need to nourish us: shopping for food also helps us feel more connected in our new home. On previous trips I remember making a point of frequenting the same shops and restaurants because I enjoyed the friendly rapport that develops when shopkeepers recognise you. It seemed you often only needed to return a second time to receive an enthusiastic welcome.

I've met other visitors here who have become loyal customers even on short stays, not just because of the quality of the food or other goods, but because they are treated like old friends. An American couple, who were our neighbours for a week, ate at the same trattoria almost every day of their visit. They had stumbled upon the place their first evening and were charmed by the owner, who looked like Liza Minnelli and made them feel right at home. Fred and Kathy treated us to a meal there one evening, and I could see how they enjoyed being greeted by name amidst joyful exclamations and kisses on both cheeks. Not only does food help soothe sadness and disappointment, celebrate victories and find its proverbial way to a man's heart, it also seems to be a natural medium for putting down roots in a foreign country, whether it's for a few days or forever.

Piazza Santo Spirito has a number of restaurants. Besides Caffé Ricchi there is Borgo Antico, perfect for a crisp pizza or one of their tasty *primi*; Cabiria for an *aperitivo* on the patio or in their funky bar or discreet back room; and Osteria Santo Spirito for the cheese gnocchi, chocolate cake, and cosy and colourful décor. Brothers from Calabria run the friendly, casual Gustapanino, just right for a quick sandwich and glass of wine, and now that they've expanded into the space next door and opened a small patio, also for *primi*, *secondi*, *dolci* and *caffè*.

A *tabacchi* is run by the same family who owns Ricchi next door. Here you can recharge your mobile phone; stock up on bus tickets; buy a lottery ticket, gum and mints, fine pens, postcards (including some of the façade projections) and tobacco. La Scartoffia, which means something along the lines of 'a confusion of paper', is a *cartoleria*, stationery store, on the south side of the piazza. The young family who runs it has crammed in school supplies, toys, party decorations and backpacks, and will also send faxes and make copies for customers. When it's time for a new notebook, Ella always looks forward to choosing her favourite cover from the stack. A few doors down, the pharmacy dispenses medicine and medical opinions. This is where I was directed for a water jug filter; considered a health-related item, it wasn't stocked at the *mesticheria*, where I naturally expected to find it. (Sometimes it feels as if I am putting together a puzzle as I try to figure out where to go for what.) The *farmacia* also sells orthopaedic slippers, face cream and plastic developmental toys, and the current window display is as seasonal as those of the produce stands, reflecting the autumnal return of *pidocchi*, or lice, which are referred to by the bizarrely affectionate term of *ospiti*—guests!—on notices in the local preschools.

It may seem challenging to revert to primitive gathering rituals when modern cities have strived so hard to exchange them for super stores that meet all our needs under one roof. Enormous supermarkets do exist in Italy, but they are located on the outskirts of the city, which means taking a bus if you are without a car, as we are. The bus system in Florence is great—if there isn't a *sciopero*, strike, or if you don't get stuck waiting by the noisy and polluted roadside for a bus that's supposed to come every six minutes but instead takes almost an hour.

Living in a place where shops are within easy walking distance has caused me to re-examine my habits of acquisition and consumption. Occasionally I will go to a real supermarket; the size of these places and the variety that I used to find overwhelming seem more enticing in limited doses. But since we don't live near the right bus stop, everything we pick up in the excitement of doing one-stop shopping hangs heavy in the bags, incising grooves on our fingers during the walk home.

Regardless of where I shop, having to carry every purchase, even partially, on foot—and then lug it up fifty-five steps—means I think more before buying and, consequently, little goes to waste. Even though I sometimes miss driving my VW Beetle with the windows down and the stereo turned up, I never really looked forward to running errands in California. I much prefer being able to walk almost everywhere, and being able to survive without the hassles of owning a car makes any perceived inconveniences worth it to me.

Picking up things seems so much simpler on foot, and every time I walk out the front door seems to be a chance for historic discoveries or cultural adventures. There's a noticeable increase of human contact, and I like how the shopkeepers in my *quartiere* often know just why I'm there. At the café in the morning, it's for a cappuccino; at Rosa's in the piazza it's for figs or mint or another seasonal favourite; at the bakery Letizia will have a loaf of *sportivo* on the scale as soon as she sees it's my turn. And there's something wonderful about being regularly addressed as *'Bella'* and *'Cara'*, and how the Italians are so generous with the word *'brava'*. I bring recycled plastic bags and brown paper sacks to the produce stands and I am told *'Brava'*; Ella rescues me when I'm struggling to communicate in Italian, and they say *'Brava'*; I have the correct change ready in a shop and I hear *'Brava'* again (they love exact change here). The confidence and self-esteem of the Italians must be positively affected by the everyday use of these words in their exchanges. It always strikes me as especially lovely when one elderly man addresses another with a jovial *'Ciao, Bello!'*

By the time we reach the apartment after visiting the market and other shops along our way, not only have we gathered enough food to get us through the next couple of days, but also ideas on how to prepare it, a number of smiles, and a glow from being called *Bella*. So while buying food involves more stops now, I recognise the distinct value added by these small interactions that contribute immeasurably to our sense of feeling at home here. And while I used to be put off by those *'non toccare'* signs that prohibit customers from touching or choosing their own produce, now I appreciate that the shopkeepers are choosing the best for me. The whole experience adds up to the luxury equivalent of shopping: at these tiny family-run establishments, someone else does the work, takes care of some of the decisions—and I feel looked after.

When it comes to shopping—with the exception of books—I enjoy the process of buying food most. It's something we always need, there's no question of size or whether it flatters the figure, it never goes out of style and it takes up a minimum of space in my small apartment. I have something nice to unwrap when I get home, and there remain before me endless possibilities.

After returning from the market I arrange the vegetables that will go into soup for dinner tonight. Each time I enter the kitchen my eye is drawn to the orange flesh of the pumpkin, the papery purple skins of red onions, the feathery tops of the fennel and the leafy *cavolo nero*, a cabbage so dark that it's called 'black'. In a brown wicker basket I compose a still life with the sunset colours of pomegranates, persimmons and new apples, then select a dark green and raw sienna bowl whose colours, if mixed together, would create the same mottled hue of the dusky golden grapes now cascading over the edge. Although I often only have time to arrange the produce quickly, in my mind I am capturing these simple shows of beauty with a paintbrush or pencil. Of course, food is also a medium in its own right, offering the opportunity to express creativity for fleeting moments of time—as a weekday dinner, a long lunch, or a gorgeous dessert.

It is at Rosa's stand in the piazza that my culinary education has been nurtured. When I decided to try making Thrice Cooked Thistle, Rosa told me how to prepare the thistle first. She inspired me to try 'melting' *peperoncini*, a type of green capsicum about the shape and size of green beans, into a lovely sauce for spaghetti. She sold me my first fresh garlic. 'What's that?' I asked, feeling mildly ignorant when she said it was simply freshly harvested garlic; I had only seen it dried before. The tenderness and bright green of her early-November spinach encouraged Ella and me to try a vegetable that we both normally dislike—and we found it to be more delicate in flavour than any spinach we had tasted before. I also credit Rosa with my daughter's love of pomegranates; it wasn't until Rosa gave her a torn off chunk of pomegranate, with its bright jewels dripping with vitamins, that Ella realised how amazing they taste. We bought a bagful and went to sit on the church steps, leaving behind a trail of red juice and a feast of fallen seeds for the birds when we got up. Who knew there was so much pleasure in a pomegranate? I can see why it symbolises abundance, fertility and good luck.

My relationship with food has undergone a fundamental change in the last decade; up until then, only baking interested me. But now, far from the days when my husband tried (unsuccessfully) to teach me when the spaghetti was *al dente*, I find myself as the only cook—and not unwillingly. Since we rarely eat out, I cook a lot, and what used to seem like a chore has become more of a meditation. It has been great fun trying out familiar ingredients with the various Italian staples—pasta, risotto, polenta, bread—and discovering and inventing new recipes. I like how a central ingredient can be stretched from one dinner to another, assuming a different form each time: porridge-like polenta with gorgonzola the first day, grilled polenta served with caramelised fennel the next, and fried on the third—or how the leaves stripped from the broccoli that I serve as a side dish one night go into soup the next day. An affinity for versatility and experimentation guides me in the kitchen, as in the other areas of my creative life.

Despite finding such pleasure in Tuscan cuisine, sometimes I crave a taste of ethnic food. Around the corner from Piazza Santo

Spirito is the Asia Market (which should more accurately be called the International Market). Here I can buy an eclectic mix of items not easily found elsewhere: Thai noodles, basmati rice, black beans for Brazilian *feijoada* stew, and dark brown sugar, dried coconut and rolled oats for chocolate chip oatmeal biscuits. It still amazes me to see how long it's possible to stay within the realm of Tuscan cooking, but somehow there's no Italian substitute for homemade avocado-tomato salsa with fresh lime. Of course I am still using the tomatoes and red onions from the market in the piazza, but without the green ingredients it would just be a topping for bruschetta, or an uncooked pasta sauce. Coriander snipped from my window box completes the Mexican-restaurant-in-southern-California experience.

I tend to use cookbooks mainly as a starting point; they serve more as a 'place' I can go, to reflect on the tips and personal experiences of the author, to dream about how the dishes might taste, to appreciate the beauty of an appealingly photographed recipe and a well laid out page. I usually look over several versions of a recipe and then interpolate the best solution for my circumstances, enjoying the process of making the recipe mine—sometimes out of necessity if I don't have all the ingredients, but often just from an instinct to personalise anything that I put my time and energy into. When I first came to Italy I didn't have room to pack a cookbook, so I bought Marcella Hazan's *Essentials of Classic Italian Cooking* to help me in the kitchen until my friend Tessa Kiros's next cookbook was due out (the gorgeous *Falling Cloudberries*). While I appreciate having access to Marcella's vast knowledge of Italian cuisine, Tessa's flexible approach towards the art of turning ingredients into a unique dish better matches my own.

Most of us are aware of the Italians' amazing relationship with food. The three-course Tuscan meals served at the Pensione Bencistà still stand out in my memory: their super-fresh ingredients, prepared simply and served as multiple courses in a leisurely manner, introduced me to a whole new way of eating. And I discovered that moderation, not deprivation, was the reigning philosophy in matters of food in Italy.

Not until enrolling my daughter at the local primary school did I truly realise just how deeply rooted is the expectation of seasonably varied, multi-course meals. I could hardly believe it when Ella brought home a full-colour poster featuring four rotating weeks of both summer and winter menus, with the organic ingredients highlighted in green ink. In the school cafeteria, tables of six are set with baskets of bread, bowls of *parmeggiano* and bottles of water, and the children are served a *primo* (soup, pasta or risotto), a *secondo* (meat, eggs or cheese) with vegetables, and *frutta di stagione* (fruit of the season) to finish off—certainly more impressive than a typical weekday lunch in my home.

It's been interesting to see how the Italian schools choose to focus their energy; a generous two hours are devoted to the midday meal and time to play. In contrast to the multi-course lunches, the play space is simply a large gravelled area without slides or swings, although the wisteria-covered pergola is lovely when it's in bloom and several old trees provide shade and hiding places. And instead of using textbooks, the students create their own within the gridded notebooks they have for each subject.

There's no doubt that dealing with the numerous uncertainties of daily life in Italy—frequent *scioperi*, piercing Vespas screeching through the streets, irregular opening hours, confusion over whether or not to pay before or after ordering your cappuccino at the bar—requires patience, humour and a flexible attitude. But the Italians' willingness to make eating more than just a refuelling experience, either as they sell you the food that you will take home to prepare, or as they feed you in their trattorias, feels like a fair trade-off. I still remember an August visit when I returned to an osteria where I had previously discovered a favourite risotto dish, flavoured with pears and gorgonzola. I noticed that the seasonably appropriate *risotto al melone*, melon risotto, had replaced it, and was quite disappointed, since I intensely dislike rockmelon. When the waiter learnt about my fond memories of the autumn version, he excused himself for a moment. Upon his return he said, 'I have this,' and as he revealed a pear in his palm he added, 'so we can make it for you.'

It's about five o'clock in the afternoon. The light, filtered through the trees, is perfect. People have placed themselves around Santo Spirito's fountain: families with gelato, or breadcrumbs for the pigeons; a student with a sketchpad; couples with their guidebooks; others just observing the scene. The father of one of Ella's classmates asks if I can keep an eye on his daughter so she can continue skipping while he runs upstairs to stir the carrots for dinner. I watch as waiters and cooks from the local restaurants join in on a casual soccer game, as do a couple of the piazza's homeless men. This is place becoming so much more than a location: layered with memory and emotion, it has become a part of me. As the seasons change, their beautiful rhythm turning too quickly into years, the experiences I hold from this piazza come together to create a living collage. It's the setting for so much life, energy, soul—not always pleasing or attractive—but authentic. Through it all, the simple plaster church façade watches over the piazza, acquiring its own sense of individuality as the years pass: Time working as Architect.

# Interlude: Piazza della Passera

While Piazza Pitti and Piazza Santo Spirito are both part of our daily lives, a third piazza also belongs to the geography of each day—Piazza della Passera. This almost incidental square possesses an enigmatic quality. Since it's not on one of the main arteries, tourists tend not to find it (unless they are lost), and I have met Florentines who have never heard of the tiny piazza. Once we moved to Piazza Pitti, it was suddenly part of our routine, as the short cut to Lory for art supplies, to the British Library to exchange the pile of books each month, to our favourite gelateria for a treat and to Ponte Santa Trìnita, a bridge we often cross to reach the other side of the river.

The piazza is also on my loop each morning after I have taken Ella to school. There's a train of greetings as I see the same classmates, parents and locals in just about the same order every day; one mother says she gauges if she and her son are on time by where our paths cross. I especially enjoy the walk at Christmas time, when many businesses place decorated trees at their entrances, tempting fate with their trust that the traffic won't knock them over, and the street that leads into Piazza della Passera is brightened by icicle lights strung overhead.

Piazza della Passera is more than another highlight of my morning journey though; the square's only café is where I stop for my first cappuccino of the day. I usually take it to the back room, which is often empty. Most customers like to stand at the bar chatting to Marco as he makes their coffee, though occasionally someone comes back here with a newspaper, or friends seek privacy as they share confidences. Sometimes I feel as if I am missing the Italian coffee bar culture by retreating to the back room—I wish I could keep up with the Italians and their sports and politics—but I enjoy listening to the rise and fall of their chatter, the bustle and the lulls.

It isn't hard to find a neighbourhood café in Florence; I have often wondered if a law mandates that there must be a coffee bar at regular intervals. Caffè degli Artigiani is not the closest one—there are four within a minute or two's walk of my apartment—but it offers exactly what I am looking for each morning. The delicious coffee and pastries, the good music, the friendly barista and the little table in the corner next to the window all combine to create an ideal second office of sorts. I often accomplish more writing and mental organising in a couple of hours here than the rest of the day, and I love beginning my day with a shot of strong coffee joined by warm milk, topped with creamy foam and served in a nicely shaped cup.

The other owner of Caffè degli Artigiani, Cinzia, is a modern day Renaissance woman: she stocks the display case with homemade treats and fills the flower vases with creative arrangements, and her excellent taste radiates throughout the café. She and Fabio (from the trattoria across the piazza) have covered most of the café's free wall space with a fascinating exhibition featuring close-up photos of faces. The concept seems simple, yet the impact is powerful—hundreds of noses, eyes and mouths in a diverse palette of skin tones, with the faces of dogs and one of a statue punctuating the exhibit with a touch of humour.

One friendly voice that carries into the back room each day is Signora Grazia's; Ella says she has laughter in her voice. I think of her as the neighbourhood spirit. She's at least a generation older than me, but seems ageless. She wears her long, dark wavy hair pulled to one side and favours strong shades of purple, red and black. Grazia loves to dance, and seems to appreciate Marco's eclectic taste in music. 'Tell me, what's better than dancing—and music?' she demands when I come to the front to pay for my coffee one morning. She answers her own question: 'Well, love … love is important too. But you have to dance.' The first time I met her she was dancing at a Christmas event in Piazza della Passera, and asked me if I wanted to join in. Since that evening we see her all over the *quartiere*: on the *sdrucciolo* as we walk to school each morning, at the market in Piazza Santo Spirito later, in the café mid-morning. Every time we go to La Mangiatoia, she's eating pizza at the counter. Sometimes I wonder if this tranquil woman who seems to float through the Oltrarno is actually one of a set of twins.

Since I started coming to this café a few years ago, I have seen toddlers growing up and new children becoming part of the neighbourhood. The local fame of one little girl who lives above the café precedes her. Bows, pink for girls and blue for boys, are placed on the main door of the palazzo when a baby is born, so long before Rebecka began making public appearances I already knew her name from the sign that accompanied her ribbon. Like so many other children, this bright-eyed little girl has become a cherished part of the piazza's story. This is where she took her first steps, where she amuses the regulars with her giggles and first words—there is a shortage of children in Italy, so they tend to draw everyone's attention—and it seems fitting that she celebrated her first birthday with a neighbourhood party at the café.

Enclosed by four- and five-storey buildings, Piazza della Passera makes me think of an intimate theatre. The height of these buildings is almost oppressive for a space of this size, but somehow it's just perfect. Performances, exhibitions and music festivals are held here throughout the year, and small galleries and artisan workshops dot each of the five narrow streets leading into the square. This spring an unsightly tower of scaffolding was constructed in the middle of the piazza, with an improvised bridge leading to a top-storey apartment that didn't have the space for scaffolding in front. In protest, a discourse about how the scaffolding must surely be an artistic statement—otherwise how could it be allowed to encroach upon the piazza like this?—was pasted on walls all over the area. As if by magic, the scaffolding disappeared just in time for the first music event of the summer.

Although its name dates back to the fourteenth century, this public outdoor space only received its official designation as Piazza della Passera in 2005. Two explanations for the long-time name have been offered, and one gives a clue as to why the answer to 'Dove siamo?' ('Where are we?') often gets a snicker—passera means 'sparrow', but is also slang for the female genitalia. Cosimo I, the first Medici to live in the nearby Palazzo Pitti, was said to have patronised a brothel here, and some say his habit inspired the nickname. The other story dates back even further, to the Black Death in 1348, when a group of youngsters tried to save an ailing sparrow. In any case, the present day piazza has been carved from the spot where the brothel once stood. Local legend says the building was bombed, and when I look for the piazza on early maps, a building does indeed occupy the current piazza; however, by 1937 the building already appeared to be gone. The reason behind the legend will probably remain another of those Italian mysteries that I so often find in the course of living here.

Mario Mariotti, the local artist who conceived the Santo Spirito façade project and designed a logo that is still used to represent the Oltrarno, kept his studio on the northern block of Via Toscanella, one of the streets that passes through the piazza. At the end of his street, Mario has recorded another piece of local history in the form of a terracotta Madonna pinching her upturned nose as a mouse runs across her hand, called *Madonna della Puzza, Madonna of the Smell*. Apparently there used to be a particularly smelly rubbish skip on the corner, although it is rumoured that dogs and people also contributed to the problem by relieving themselves there.

The tradition of creativity continues. All through the morning, *artigiani* from the local workshops stop in for a quick caffè, and by mid-morning several of the neighbourhood artists are seated in the narrow Via Toscanella alongside the café—a couple of painters, a poet, a photographer, a glass bead artist. This little summer patio is also popular for *aperitivi*, when the sun has retreated and many of the morning customers reappear.

Not only is my daily café in Piazza della Passera, but so too is a trattoria where I can always count on a really good meal: Quattro Leoni. It's listed in every guidebook—that's how I found it on my first visit to Florence—but the quality of the food has remained amazing in all the years I have been coming here. Their signature *primo* is *fiocchetti alle pere con salsa di taleggio e asparagi*, little pasta 'packages' of pear, taleggio cheese and asparagus, which is unique, but for a *primo* I usually try one of the dishes the cooks have concocted that day. Whatever the season, I order the same *secondo: tagliata di pollo*—a perfectly grilled chicken thigh served with a wedge of lemon, a little olive oil and a pile of rocket.

From spring until autumn, Quattro Leoni's dining patio adds a lot of magic to the piazza. The stars of Bethlehem—which you can watch being made in a workshop just down the street—lend a festive air on warm nights, and it's an ideal spot for diners with children: they can venture into the piazza with their games, while the adults linger over wine or dessert (always the cheesecake for me).

I learnt a new phrase today—*danza di ventre*. My enormous Italian dictionary had 'belly', 'gut' and references to 'bowels' and 'underbellies' listed for *ventre*, but only when I googled it did I realise that I had overlooked the obvious: we were in for an evening of belly dancing in Piazza della Passera. The occasion is a *notte bianca*—a white night—when the city organises an event. Many of the piazzas and streets on our side of the river are closed to traffic; people relax with friends and wander around the neighbourhood, checking out the variety of entertainment, which will go on into the wee hours.

It feels like one of those perfect evenings in Piazza della Passera. The flavours of mint and lime in a mojito refresh me as I listen to a fusion of jazz and blues with international influences. The quartet is made up of a barefoot clarinettist and an older contrabassist who smokes as he plays, while the guitarist, also barefoot, keeps his eyes closed as he strums his guitar. He looks as though he may be in another world—or perhaps he's trying to remember the notes? The laid-back drummer holds their sound together. Later on in the night, the belly dancers get a lot of attention, especially from the men in the audience. My daughter and her friend are riveted the entire time, enthralled by the sparkly costumes, the exotic music and the rhythmic wiggles of the dancers.

It would have been fun to visit all the celebrations for the *notte bianca*, discovering what they each had to offer, but Piazza della Passera feels like the right choice for tonight. I know that each morning as I approach the café, I will remember looking up at the shape of the sky created by the rooflines that define the volume of the square ... sprinkled with stars, resonating with music ... and the boundaries of the intimate piazza—the very streets leading into it—filled with people and motion.

The Piazzas of Florence

# Piazzetta Ponte Vecchio

*Along with the Duomo's cupola, Ponte Vecchio is the city's most recognisable symbol—both the clichéd subject of postcards and an historic treasure with an intriguing story. My introduction to Ponte Vecchio came in 1983, when my parents sent me one of the ubiquitous postcards. The little buildings perched off the side of the pedestrian bridge, the people clustered at the middle, appealed to my imagination. I had never seen anything like this before—the bridges I knew from Saint Louis, my hometown at the time, were enormous structures, devoid of personality, and took a couple of minutes to cross by car.*

*When I received the postcard over two decades ago, little did I know that one day crossing this bridge would be part of my daily routine. It was on the route to my daughter's school during the first few months we lived in Florence, and despite being a twenty-minute walk instead of the five-minute one we enjoy now, I liked crossing Ponte Vecchio several times each day. Mornings were best: we would often arrive at the bridge just after the street cleaner, so the stone paving was clean and glistening, the river peaceful and the road relatively empty.*

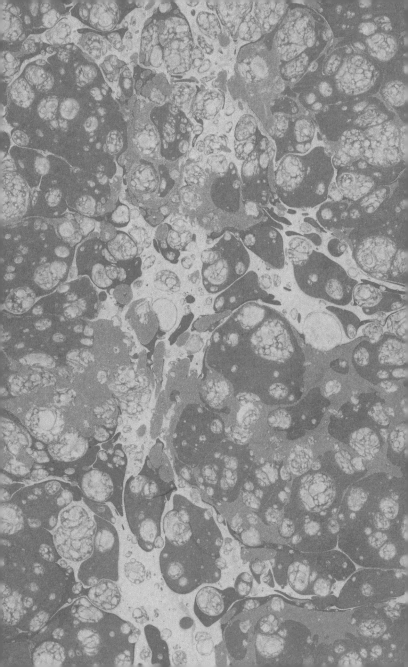

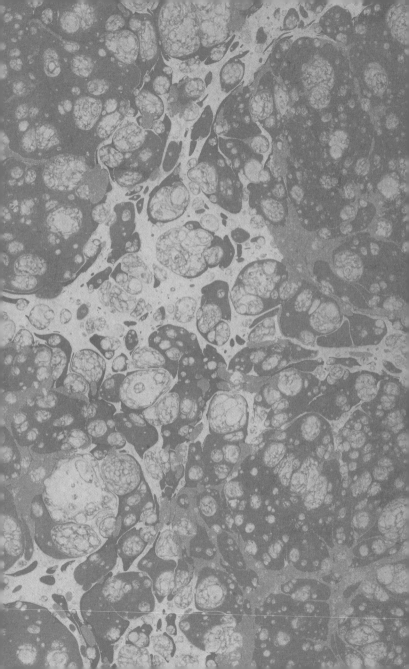

It's possible to not even realise you are on a bridge—when approached from either end, Ponte Vecchio seems like just another charming and crowded street lined with jewellery shops. Yet this dynamic link between the city's two sides is so much more than a shopping destination: its initial appeal for me was for the *place* it is. I have a bank of enticing images from all those crossings: that of the narrow wooden shopfronts framing the sparkling jewellery, each shop with its own picture window overlooking the river; the tiny wrought-iron balconies brightened by geraniums; the closed weathered shutters, concealing stories for the imagination behind them; an upper-storey sundial marking the sun's passage on one corner. But the best part of the bridge is the *piazzetta* at Ponte Vecchio's midpoint, where a gap in the two rows of shops reveals the meandering view carved out by the Arno. On a map, I find the river to be one of Florence's most interesting features, and the welcome pause it offers in the midst of this heavily paved city is similar to the relief the piazzas give to its dense city blocks.

The Arno has always been an important facet of the city's personality. In Roman times a port on the Arno controlled what was already an important crossroad. The narrowness of the river at this point allowed it to be easily bridged, which is one reason why the Romans chose to settle here. While they initially relied on a ferry, eventually they constructed a wooden bridge slightly upstream from the present day Ponte Vecchio; for many centuries they had to build a new bridge every time a flood carried it away.

Land along the river—and therefore the river itself—was finally included within the late twelfth-century circuit of walls; with the river finally a physical part of the city, Florence naturally began to expand towards the area south of the river. Later, the river's ideal position for cleaning and dying textiles would be instrumental in the success of Florence's wool and silk industries: it gave the mills their source of energy and completed the commercial circle by providing the means for transporting goods in and out of the city. The Arno lost its formerly active role when the cloth industry deserted its banks and the *lungarni* were built, creating an obstacle between the people and the river. But it may soon be assuming a new role; plans to use the Arno as a renewable and non-polluting source of energy are currently in the works.

The very nature of a river contains an inherent paradox: it provides a connection between its source and destination, as well as to other towns along its path. But a river can also create a barrier between the two parts of the city, either physically in the absence of a link from one side to the other, or psychologically even if there is one. Florence's bridges have been an integral feature of the city all along; not only did they serve as links to the area on the other side of the Arno, but their shops and chapels, meeting and viewing points also played a vital role in the citizens' everyday lives. The bridges were places with colourful and vital histories of their own, and their human scale helped to preserve a successful and intimate relationship between Florence's two sides.

Crossing the river still feels like a bit of an event to me. I love how the bridges link us so easily to the north side of the city, and how the bridges each have a view of the others. I don't necessarily need to cross the river every day, but often there is a specific reason to do so: on Thursdays for the plant market in Piazza della Repubblica; on Saturday evenings for a *passeggiata*, which often finds us sitting under the loggia in Piazza della Signoria; on a winter Sunday to stroll along the sunny northern *lungarni*, the roads that run alongside the river. There are errands to take care of on the other side of the river: visiting one of the many bookstores or specialty food shops, paying bills at the central post office, picking up a lipstick. Sunset is always a perfect time to walk to one of the bridges; you would think there are only so many photos one could take from the same spot, but my collage of sunsets reflected onto the river attests to the seemingly infinite possibilities.

In 1206 the *Opus Pontis* was established to maintain a wooden bridge that was more or less on the site of today's Ponte Vecchio. The organisation was also in charge of renting out the bridge's shops, whose earliest tenants were in the business of producing leather goods. While these days visitors are content to linger on the bridge, back when hides were left to soak for months in the Arno—and the main curing agent was horse urine—people must have felt differently.

During the course of the thirteenth century, Florence gained three additional bridges to accommodate its expansion towards the east and west and onto the other side of the river; together with Ponte Vecchio, they would serve the city's needs for the next six centuries. The first of the three new bridges was built in 1220, at the point where the 1173 walls met the river towards the west (the same site as the current Ponte alla Carraia). Officially named after the Carraia city gate, at the time it was simply called *il ponte nuovo*, 'the new bridge'; this was when Ponte Vecchio became known as the 'old bridge'. Its pronounced curves gave Ponte alla Carraia the nickname *'ponte gobbo'*—'hunchback bridge'. Besides allowing for the passage of carts carrying wool to and from San Frediano, where many of the workers lived, it also served as a viewing point for shows staged on boats floating in the river. In 1304 the bridge collapsed as enthusiastic crowds watched a performance of Dante's *Inferno*. (One can only imagine how the superstitious citizens reacted to what was surely seen as a punishment from God.)

Ella and I associate the Carraia bridge with gelato; our favourite gelateria in the city sits at its south-western corner. Many of my daughter's classmates have been coming here since they were old enough to eat ice cream, and since Gelateria La Carraia is near the primary school, it's a popular gathering spot in the late afternoon. Pistacchio is my usual choice—and also a reliable indicator of the general quality of an establishment's gelato: if the pistacchio is a bright green, it means that artificial flavours and colours have probably been used, while a dull shade of green ensures a more natural flavour.

The original version of Ponte alle Grazie was named Ponte Rubaconte after the *Podestà*, the governing magistrate, who laid its first stone in 1237. This bridge is about as far to the east of Ponte Vecchio as Ponte alla Carraia is to the west. Oratories were perched on each of its piers, and the bridge's name was changed to Ponte alle Grazie because of one in particular—Santa Maria delle Grazie. Along with other small houses, workshops and tabernacles, the oratory was dismantled in 1874 in order to widen the bridge, and then later reconstructed on the nearby *lungarno*. The present bridge, larger yet, was built to replace the one destroyed in World War II.

On 24 June, midsummer's night, we head to Ponte alle Grazie to watch the fireworks that fill the sky in honour of the feast day of San Giovanni, Florence's patron saint. The city's tradition of celebrating holidays with fireworks displays dates back several centuries. As well as being credited with inventing a unique type of sorbet-gelato in the sixteenth century, multi-talented architect Bernardo Buontalenti was also famous for creating elaborate fireworks. In his day, the San

Giovanni fireworks were set off from the top of the loggia in Piazza della Signoria. Houses were continually catching fire though, so the show was finally moved near the Arno, where another advantage is seeing the bursts of colour reflected onto the river.

The Ponte Vecchio we cross now dates back to a 1345 design by Taddeo Gaddi and Neri di Fioravante, and was built to replace a twelfth-century bridge destroyed in the exceptionally bad flood of 1333. Stone shops were added soon after the bridge's completion, and for two centuries the river was at the mercy of the produce- and meat-sellers, who dumped their refuse in it. There were also blacksmiths, with their dusty work; linen merchants, who even today have a presence on the road leading from the bridge to the north; and hosiers, who can now be found displaying pretty underthings on nearly every block in *Centro*. With an eye towards cleaning up the bridge—and with the additional benefit of collecting higher rents—Grand Duke Ferdinando I evicted them all in 1593. He invited goldsmiths and silversmiths to take over the shops, which is why a bust of Benvenuto Cellini gazes out over the river at the bridge's midpoint; Cellini's work as a goldsmith was highly regarded in the sixteenth century.

During the German retreat on 3 August 1944, Ponte Vecchio was the only old bridge spared; the others, which had finally each been built soundly enough to withstand destruction from floods, were all blown up during the bombing that lasted until dawn the next day. One legend maintains that Hitler had developed a fondness for Ponte Vecchio during a past visit, and therefore instructed his troops to leave it intact, although it seems more likely that orders to blow it up were ignored. Recently a new plaque went up in the loggia under the Vasari Corridor, in commemoration of Gerhard Wolf, the German consul to Florence during the war. He is credited with saving not only Ponte Vecchio, but also many lives and countless works of art. In any case, destroying the bridge was pointless, as even the mass of its shattered stone would still have allowed passage to the other side. Unfortunately, buildings at either end of Ponte Vecchio were dynamited, and from an architectural point of view, the streets leading from the bridge suffered a great loss. The city blocks were rebuilt with structures of a modern design, and while they can't help but stand out against the older architecture, their reflections on the river blend in quite well.

I like to stand in Ponte Vecchio's *piazzetta* in the early hours, before it swarms with people. This is when the seagulls perform, swooping and gliding across the water, and on the sunniest of mornings the Arno glitters like the Las Vegas strip. The spectacle is all the more lovely because of the view of the handsome Ponte Santa Trìnita. The Santa Trìnita bridge we gaze at today is actually the result of a painstaking reconstruction of a sixteenth-century design by Ammannati, undertaken after the bridge was blown up in 1944. Ponte Santa Trìnita owes its frequently used epithet of 'most beautiful bridge' to the trio of graceful arches, which became the defining feature after a flood in 1557 necessitated a new structure. Curiously, the arches have no mathematical derivation, but they share the same curve as the bases upon which Michelangelo's sculptures of *Night*, *Day*, *Dawn* and *Dusk* recline in the New Sacristy of San Lorenzo. Indeed, Michelangelo's collaboration meant he should also have taken some credit for Santa Trìnita's design.

The bridge was originally built in 1252 as a means of linking the Oltrarno and the church of Santa Trìnita, and it was lined with small houses, shops and votive chapels for travellers, as were the other bridges. Although Ponte Santa Trìnita is very different to Ponte Vecchio now—there are no little buildings, no widening of the footpath, no ban on traffic—the bridge does enjoy the character of a piazza to some extent. Brave teenagers venture onto the parapets, people congregate all along the low wall, especially at sunset: taking photographs, lost in thought, sharing a romantic moment. During the cocktail hour, customers from a bar on the adjacent *lungarno* take their *aperitivi* across the street for a riverside view, while artists sometimes set up their impromptu open-air studios along the wall.

Someday I would like to create a mosaic of the Arno, using the many images I have captured on film. I look forward to its ever-changing colours, how the river serves as a canvas: throughout the day, as the light changes and the weather's mood affects the sky and the buildings, the water's reflections are transformed. The wind plays with the texture of the river, sometimes turning the water stormy, other times rippling it softly. At its worst, the river's colour reminds me of a cold cup of weak milky tea, but other times it will assume a striking shade of bright olive-green, a bold breathtaking blue or a mysterious deep mercury.

While it's certainly no wildlife reserve, a surprising variety of small creatures are attracted to the river. So are Ella and I. We keep our eyes open for the nutria, a water rat-like creature that glides through the river and creeps along its banks. Swallows circle in the morning and bats swoop in the evening. Sometimes huge fish swim around Ponte Vecchio's piers, rewarded with crumbs from tourists. We often see ducks paddling through the water or on the sandy shore, and this spring one flew low over the bridge, thrillingly close to our heads. He must have fallen behind, out of formation. Once Ella spotted a turtle swimming with the current. As we discussed how long it would take for him to reach the sea, we saw the turtle (wisely, in our estimation) make a ninety-degree turn and head for the shore.

Ponte Vecchio retained its symmetrical organisation until 1565, when the Vasari Corridor was built at Cosimo I's request. The occasion for the enclosed corridor that ran above the shops on the east side of Ponte Vecchio was Francesco I's marriage to Giovanna d'Austria; Vasari had just five months to complete the structure. The elaborate Medici decorations for festivities were often removed after an event, but Cosimo I had another, permanent, motive for this structure: he wanted to be able to enjoy a safe, comfortable—and private—walk from Palazzo Pitti as he crossed over to Palazzo Vecchio, where Francesco lived and government affairs were run until the *uffizi* (the new government offices) were ready.

I like to follow the corridor's course as I walk from Piazza Pitti to Piazza della Signoria; it winds through the city overhead, through some buildings and around others. The grand dukes would have left Palazzo Pitti and passed through the long block along Via de' Guicciardini to Piazza Santa Felicita, where the corridor emerges to run along the façade of the church. A point of access onto a balcony overlooking the nave allowed members of the Medici family to participate in mass without being seen. Next the corridor disappears inside a building, then reappears to cross the road overhead before narrowing to cantilever off the side of the Torre dei Mannelli; the family stubbornly refused to have their tower destroyed to make way for the passage. After crossing the river above Ponte Vecchio's shops, the corridor turns right at Piazza del Pesce and continues above a riverside loggia until it reaches the Uffizi.

For three centuries the grand dukes and their entourage used this passage to cross the river. The corridor then opened to the public in the twentieth century, but had to be closed for almost a decade due to damage during World War II, and again after the 1966 flood. In 1993, a bomb at the Uffizi destroyed part of the corridor and some of the art, which caused yet another closure. Even now, it's not easy to get a reservation for a tour of the Vasari Corridor, but I was once able to experience what it was like to 'go home' to Piazza Pitti via the private route. Lining the walls is the artwork of Italian and French artists, a vast collection of artists' self-portraits through the centuries (including Carlo Levi's, the artist and writer who lived in my building for a time) and a number of Medici portraits. But the real stars are the views overlooking the streets, the river and the *piazzetta*, and the glimpses of private gardens tucked behind the city blocks.

Mark Twain thought the Arno a stream so small that he wondered why the Florentines needed bridges at all. 'Why should they think themselves too good to wade?' he asked facetiously in his book, *Pictures of Italy*.

While it's true that the river could dry up in the summer, the Arno has expressed its dangerous side repeatedly over the centuries.

The worst of the modern day floods inundated the city in 1966, damaging and destroying a heartbreaking amount of artwork and property. The river assumed a different kind of role then—unifying the city on a spiritual level, as both residents and international neighbours pitched in to return Florence to normal.

So in November 2006, with great enthusiasm, the city celebrated its recovery from the flood forty years earlier. The *lungarni* became exhibition spaces for photographs showing the condition of the riverbanks after the flood, and a rainbow of coloured lights illuminated Ponte Vecchio every night until the New Year. An exhibition of work by American photojournalist David Lees filled the Sala d'Arme in Palazzo Vecchio; the documents and books hung to dry in every available cloister and courtyard provided a theme for some impressive photographic compositions. It seems that the whole city was turned into a restoration workshop.

On the anniversary date, the footage of amateur films and slide shows, accompanied by a soundtrack of rushing water, were projected onto the walls of the Loggia dei Lanzi in Piazza della Signoria. An unusual simulation of the flood was orchestrated down by the river: Ponte Vecchio hovered in an eerie mist as a virtual net of lasers undulated through the air, rising higher by the moment. I could imagine the water rising that awful night—heavy, suffocating—and felt as if I too were being submerged by the river. The weightless, intangible lasers succeeded in recalling the horror and recreating the sense of panic in a surprisingly powerful way.

So many different bridges have spanned the river through the city's history; each of those within the old centre can boast had multiple versions. The idea of designing a bridge holds a lot of appeal for me, partly because a bridge is such a dynamic element, a great metaphor. A bridge can traverse water, canyons, roads, buildings; it can link two geographical places or cultures. I consider the possibilities: there could be a garden or an outdoor café—the bridge could float upon the river. It could acknowledge the past or not, be aimed at pedestrians or a high-velocity train. Maybe a bold design would be the most important feature. As I pause on Ponte Santa Trìnita and look across at Ponte Vecchio, I try to imagine how it would be if the bridge had been glassed in, with new iron storefronts and lit by chandeliers, as one architect from the 1850s had in mind. Fortunately the design wasn't implemented (save for a single shopfront) and the connection between bridge and river was preserved; crossing Ponte Vecchio wouldn't be the same experience if you couldn't feel the sun and fresh air, the wind and rain.

After Ponte Santa Trìnita was blown up in World War II, there was talk of rebuilding it with a modern design that would reference but not replicate Ammannati's, which had withstood the elements for close to four hundred years. Perhaps having learnt from past mistakes made in the name of urban 'revitalisation' or 'modernisation', the city decided instead to rebuild Santa Trìnita exactly as before, and in as authentic a manner as possible. Old tools came out, the same quarry that had been used in the Boboli Garden was reopened, the original plans were consulted. It is fortunate that Ponte Vecchio survived the war; while rebuilding Ponte Santa Trìnita was possible, the layers of time superimposed over its stone structure make Ponte Vecchio irreplaceable—without them it would no longer be *the* Ponte Vecchio.

After managing for several hundred years with those first links, two new bridges joined Florence's original four in the 1830s. The combined effects of war, disease and floods had kept the population from increasing at the rate that had originally been projected, so the city was only just beginning to grow beyond the confines of its final circle of walls. Grand Duke Leopoldo, who was particularly interested in the fields of science and engineering, wanted to showcase the latest technology by commissioning two suspension bridges—Ponte San Ferdinando and Ponte San Leopoldo (now replaced by Ponte San Niccolò and Ponte alla Vittoria, respectively). I used to think Ponte San Niccolò rather plain in comparison to Ponte Vecchio and Santa Trìnita, but I appreciate its design more since I noticed how the single swooping curve mimics the undulating hills in the distance.

Five more bridges have been built since the post-war reconstruction period that put the first six back into service. In one of the latest changes to the urban scheme, a new bridge will convey the first of the much-disputed *tramvia* routes through Le Cascine (a long green park over to the west of town) and across to the south side of the river. The design attempts to continue the tradition of the human-scaled link between both sides by also providing a bike lane and a pedestrian passage.

People always seem to want to get closer to the river. Although the river banks are nothing like the bustling places we see portrayed in paintings from the days when the cloth workers used it daily, the weirs are often full of sunbathers in warm weather; Ponte alle Grazie shelters fishermen; and the rowing club attracts members who slide through the river on sleek sculls that bear no resemblance to the rather ramshackle vessels that used to populate the Arno. A public summer beach has only just opened between Ponte alle Grazie and Ponte San Niccolò. While bathing won't be safe for several more years, the people can begin to re-establish their relationship with the river ... a step in the right direction after the *lungarni* and the embankments have created such a formal barrier between the city and the Arno for so long.

Sometimes I avoid coming to Ponte Vecchio because the bridge can be so jammed with people, although it's almost worth it just to watch the local cyclists matter-of-factly negotiate their way through the crowds. This morning Ella and I are blowing bubbles from the *piazzetta*, curious to see if they will float on the river or disappear before reaching the water. (They float.) I notice a small elderly man, dressed in a fine hat and blazer, dusting off the windows of his jewellery shop. With the opening hour fast approaching, the bridge is full of proprietors sweeping, hosing down the footpath, cleaning their shopfronts—a typical morning scene before the bridge grows crowded, at which point the owners will seek sanctuary in their shops. Overhead, the birds perform their usual early morning fly-bys, squawking as if in protest as traffic rattles along the *lungarni*. Sunlight sparkles on the river, and I imagine sprinkling a handful of glitter on a map—it would be a perfect expression of the river's meandering journey through the city today.

# Piazza della Signoria

Considered by many residents to be the most beautiful piazza in Florence—some say in Italy, even the world—Piazza della Signoria's irregular boundaries seem to hold the heart of the city within them, embracing and relinquishing the bustle and commotion of the endless number of residents and visitors who traverse the square several times each day. Florentines still lament the loss of the red-brick paving, which was replaced by grey stone after the archaeological excavations of the Roman city below, but it's a relief that this piazza is no longer a parking lot for cars and tour buses as it was a few decades ago.

The busy pedestrian Via dei Calzaiuoli links Piazza della Signoria and Piazza del Duomo, joining the city's civic heart with its religious centre. As the primary functions of the piazzas differ, so too do their characters. While Piazza del Duomo flows around its focal point—the cathedral—Piazza della Signoria is a large open area, with edges defined by the buildings: the piazza and its activity become the focus. The most important feature, Palazzo Vecchio, appears to step in from one corner of the square, and its ninety-five metre bell tower providing the civic counterpoint to the colourful, ornately patterned one designed by Giotto for the Duomo.

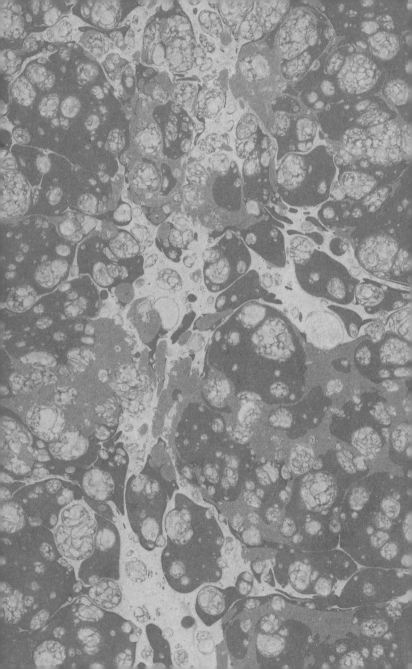

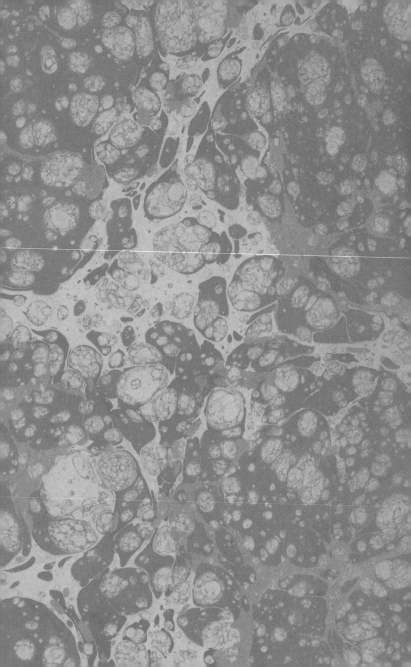

My natural impulse varies with each of these piazzas. When I go to Piazza del Duomo, I like to enter the cathedral or climb high above it, to be right at the centre of the city. In Piazza della Signoria my inclination is to find a spot somewhere around the edge—under the loggia, on the steps in front of Palazzo Vecchio, on Caffè Rivoire's patio—and look into the middle of the piazza, which is like a big container for people and energy.

A favourite ritual when I visit the piazza includes first stopping off at a nearby sandwich bar, I Fratellini, where I pick up a *numero uno*, a sandwich of prosciutto, rocket and goat's cheese on a warm, crusty roll. It's always fun to join the crowd hovering around the wooden shelves on the wall, which give customers a spot to set down their glasses of wine as they eat. But more often than not, I walk the couple of short blocks back to Piazza della Signoria and find a free bit of kerb where I can sit and watch the chaotic mixture of locals, visitors, children, dogs, horses and pigeons that doesn't change much from one day to another, but always entertains me.

Afterwards I have a quick *caffè macchiato*, an espresso 'stained' with milk, at Rivoire's bar. Rivoire is known for its unrivalled spot on the piazza as well as its distinctive hot chocolate. A cold and drizzly evening after Christmas shopping always seems the perfect time to indulge in a *cioccolata* with fresh cream. Once in a while, on one of those warm evenings when the days are long and stretch towards ten o'clock, I take a seat on the patio and splurge on a flute of bubbly prosecco, which is accompanied by a plate of salty snacks and a more dignified seat than I usually choose in the piazza.

But wherever you sit, there are reminders that Florence's history was written in this square. The stones we walk across now pave an area that was once the property of the Uberti family. During the period of conflict between the Guelphs (the pro-Papacy faction) and the Ghibellines (the pro-Holy Roman Empire faction), the rival families of each of these political groups took turns destroying the towers and homes of their enemies while they were in exile. The two factions alternately dominated the city in the thirteenth century, but the Guelphs won a decisive battle at Benevento in 1266, and assumed control from that point on. A couple of years later, the Uberti property was demolished, making it clear that the Ghibelline family's exile was permanent. Legend has it that future building was prohibited on this site, so from this first corner the piazza began to grow, developing an asymmetrical shape. The general lack of symmetry has allowed a unique character to settle over the square: Palazzo Vecchio assumed a rather unceremonious position in relationship to the irregularly shaped piazza, and the bell tower was not centred within the façade because its placement relied upon the existing foundations of one of the old family towers.

Citizens witnessed and participated in a variety of events in Piazza della Signoria. The revolt of the *ciompi* took place here in 1378, when the poorer class of wool-workers fought to have a voice in the government by establishing their own guilds. An especially powerful image handed down through the centuries is Leonardo da Vinci's sketch of a corpse hanging from one of Palazzo Vecchio's windows: one of the men involved in the unsuccessful Pazzi Conspiracy in 1478. The Bonfire of the Vanities, instigated in this piazza by the austere preacher Girolamo Savonarola in 1497, was followed by his own demise in a bonfire in Piazza della Signoria the next year. For centuries, a celebration was held here on San Giovanni's feast day, and colourful fireworks filled the square. The French took over the piazza when they entered Florence as the new rulers in 1799, and then just a few months later, the Florentines rebelled by burning the symbols of the republic. Michelangelo's original sculpture of *David* created a stir as it began a five-day journey north to the Accademia in 1873. And in just one of many political rallies and demonstrations, Mussolini, accompanied by Hitler, spoke to huge crowds from the balcony of Palazzo Vecchio in 1940.

Since I have been living in Florence, the piazza seems to host only events of a positive nature: floats converge in a massive party at the end of the *Carnevale* parade; the piazza fills with crowds partaking in the celebration of the *vendemmia*, the grape harvest; public concerts commemorate local and national holidays; and Florentines dressed in historical costumes parade through the piazza during their festive processions.

As the centuries passed, the piazza's name evolved to reflect the city's current political rulers. First known as Piazza dei Priori, it later became Piazza dei Signori or della Signoria, after the members of the government (who occupied the civic *palazzo* that also changed names with the same frequency as its occupants). It became Piazza Ducale when Cosimo I was named duke, and then Piazza del Granduca when he, and then Florence's subsequent leaders, were granted the title of Grand Duke. During the brief Napoleonic rule, it was mockingly called Piazza Nazionale, and finally, after the unification of Italy in the 1860s, it returned to its former name, Piazza della Signoria.

The piazza is never truly empty: a varied group of statues fills the piazza, each one telling the story of a character forever frozen in stone. A copy of *David* stands to one side of Palazzo Vecchio's entrance, casting its recognisable shadow onto the rough stone

Piazza della Signoria

wall. *Hercules and Cacus* by Baccio Bandinelli balances *David*'s bulk to the right of the entrance, while a copy of *Judith and Holofernes*, with Judith triumphantly holding Holofernes's head, stands to *David*'s left. Each figure represents a political reference that changed over time, depending on the statue's location and who was in charge of the city. *Judith and Holofernes*, for example, had been commissioned by Cosimo il Vecchio for the courtyard of the Medici home north of the Duomo, but later the Florentines put her in Piazza della Signoria as a symbol of their republican ideals. The definitive return of the Medici in 1530 squashed those dreams; when Cosimo I came to power it marked the beginning of another two centuries of Medici rule. The first grand duke is portrayed in Giambologna's grand equestrian statue, which is poised mid-gallop in the middle of the piazza.

At one corner of Palazzo Vecchio, Ammannati's *Neptune*, surrounded by nymphs, tritons and horses, rises out of the centre of a fountain; this is probably the most flamboyant of Florence's typically restrained fountains. And just as the horses belonging to the police and the carriage-owners mimic the stone and bronze horses, reminders of the real lions that were once kept as symbols of strength and liberty—heraldic *marzocchi*—are found at various points around the square. The lions also gave their name to Via dei Leoni, which runs along the east side of the palace, where their cages used to be.

Adjacent to Palazzo Vecchio, a monumental three-vault loggia shelters an open-air museum of sculpture that dates from Roman times to the nineteenth century. The Loggia dei Lanzi serves as a sort of pivot point between Piazza della Signoria and the long, narrow Piazzale degli Uffizi that extends south towards the river. Its slightly raised position makes it an ideal place to sit and observe both the everyday goings-on and the many special events that happen here throughout the year.

The Piazzas of Florence

Built in the 1370s, the Loggia dei Lanzi was constructed with a more open and less imposing character than had been necessary when building Palazzo Vecchio a century earlier. The loggia's function changed during the centuries: while its original purpose had been to provide a covered outdoor space where city officials could conduct public ceremonies, it also became a place where residents could seek respite from the weather, or gather for informal meetings when the loggia wasn't in use for public events. It acquired the name Loggia dei Lanzi in the sixteenth century, when Cosimo I stationed the Swiss lancers here to guard the square.

Many of the statues in the loggia were created at a time when sculpture was being freed from the confines of niches, and was intended to be appreciated from all angles. Benvenuto Cellini's *Perseus* and Giambologna's *The Rape of the Sabine Women* are two of the most notable. These and the other statues dating from the Renaissance onwards contrast dramatically with the originals and copies from antiquity, which are serenely lined up against the back wall. Next to the Renaissance statues, which convey a wonderful sense of movement as one walks around them, they seem almost two-dimensional.

Not long after the completion of the first government building in 1252—the Palazzo del Popolo, what we now know as the Bargello— plans were already being made for a grander structure that would shift the civic heart of the city slightly west, positioning it on the same axis as the religious centre. The new *palazzo*, called Palazzo dei *Priori*, was begun in 1299, and soon after it became the residence and meeting place for the *Priori*, a group of nine men who were in charge of the city for two-month terms. The *Priori* would be sequestered at the palace during this period (theoretically to cut them off from outside influences and distractions), but as compensation they received luxurious meals and nights of entertainment.

The impenetrable exterior of the palace, which later became known as Palazzo Vecchio, is not surprising; it acknowledged the government's need to protect itself from the populace as well as from rival cities. The design served as a model for several other city halls built in medieval times, so it's interesting to note how different it is to Palazzo Ducale in Venice. Built just a few decades later, the rose and white marble façade of the Venetian civic palace is much lighter and more carefree in feeling—a result of its geographical position and the political confidence Venice enjoyed at the time.

In the 1320s a *ringhiera*, a raised platform that offered a safe place for haranguing, was added along the west side of Palazzo Vecchio. Also used for official public addresses and ceremonies before the Loggia dei Lanzi was built, it somewhat softened the fortress-like appearance of the building. But when the Florentines asked the Duke of Athens to be their ruler in 1342, his paranoia led him to reinforce the *palazzo* with yet more fortifications. No trace remains of them now: the Florentines removed the duke's additions once they ousted the tyrant less than ten months later.

Palazzo Vecchio's entrance used to be on the north side, where the hotchpotch appearance of this meandering façade offers clues to the many subsequent additions made to the building's original rectangular section. The northern door leads into the Sala d'Arme, the Room of Arms, where some wonderful temporary exhibitions are now held, while the entrance to the palace's museum is on the western façade. Visitors enter through a courtyard surrounded by columns, which look as if they are piped with icing, and frescoes showing Austrian cities and landscapes, added to welcome Francesco I's new wife, Giovanna d'Austria, in 1565.

Upstairs are the grand rooms where government affairs were conducted, as well as the former private rooms of the Medici, who lived here after moving from Palazzo Medici and before retreating to Palazzo Pitti. After walking through the first floor and the Quartiere degli Elementi on the second, you can step onto a corner terrace, the Terrazza di Saturno, for a breath of fresh air and a view of the Uffizi, Santa Croce, San Miniato and the hillside beyond. Along the Via della Ninna below are columns and other reminders of the old church of San Pietro Scheraggio, which was demolished when the Uffizi was built.

Down the hall from the *terrazza* is the Quartiere di Eleonora, where Cosimo I's wife stayed until she decided to move the family to the more spacious setting of Palazzo Pitti. Several frescoes give a flavour for the celebrations that were once held in the city's major squares. Also on this floor is the Sala delle Carte Geografiche; although not a large and impressive room like many of the others, for me it's one of the highlights of Palazzo Vecchio. Cabinets lining the walls are painted with dozens of maps from the second half of the sixteenth century, showing the extent of the known world at that time, and a large globe sits in the middle of the room.

My fascination with maps has no doubt been passed on from my father. He started collecting and writing about antique maps a couple of decades ago and has become an independent scholar of cartography since retiring from his career in international business. I have had the pleasure of seeing some of these old maps and atlases up close. They are works of art; sometimes the places featured are shown in perspective view, or a series of drawings of the city's landmarks frames the map. Even the details have such integrity—the compass rose, the scale, the lettering, the web of navigational lines. This enjoyment of maps is linked to my admiration for architectural drawings, beginning with the floor plan. While the plan view can be inherently limiting—it is so incomplete—an aesthetically pleasing plan provides a good starting point from which to extend into three dimensions. The older buildings, with their thick walls and solid columns, had such presence on paper even before they were built.

Wandering around these palatial buildings, with their layers of history—frescoes, statues, architectural details, all important and interesting for one reason or another—can be overwhelming, bringing to mind the so-called Stendhal's Syndrome. French writer Stendhal wrote about feeling faint and dizzy from the quantity and the beauty of the art that he encountered on a visit to Florence in 1817, and in 1979 his name was chosen to label similar experiences. I have heard that each year a dozen or so people actually end up in the hospital, diagnosed with Stendhal's Syndrome. While this sounds quite melodramatic, part of me can relate to the possibility after visiting many of Florence's museums and churches.

Going out to the Loggia dei Lanzi to watch the activity in the piazzas is always a good antidote to Stendhal-like symptoms. I'm not sure if it's being outdoors or just the act of remaining stationary for a little while after all the grandeur of Palazzo Vecchio, but this is an ideal place to absorb the atmosphere of the two piazzas—especially when one of the Polish musicians is strumming his guitar in Piazzale degli Uffizi. Street musicians often set up at the intersection of the two piazzas or under the arcade that runs along the Uffizi, their instrument cases sprinkled with loose change, confirming the appeal of music as a universal language.

Piazzale degli Uffizi carves a strong line from the south-eastern corner of Piazza della Signoria, with the Uffizi's repeating rhythm of columns and sculptures of famous Florentines leading the eye towards the river at its end. Artists, street performers and illegal vendors all vie for attention in this courtyard-like space, where works of sculpture are often exhibited. The queue under the loggia is an ever-present feature, commonly growing to a four-hour wait. (Luckily I discovered the benefits of the Amici degli Uffizi membership, which allows admission to the Uffizi via a special entrance, as well as free entrance to all state museums.)

The U-shaped Uffizi, conceived to house the government offices of the Medici family, now showcases a world-renowned selection of drawings, paintings and sculpture. This building by Vasari also affords a wonderful experience in perspective and views, including a chance to gaze down at the activity along the river. From the patio of the café, which sits on top of the Loggia dei Lanzi, you can see Palazzo Vecchio's bell tower up close and the city's rooftops stretching to the north.

So many masterpieces grace the walls of the Uffizi. There are the early depictions of the Madonna, which show the progression from iconic to expressive; the works by Botticelli, hung in the large wooden-trussed hall that was once part of the theatre; the portraits of members of the Medici family in the octagonal tribuna. I always think of the Uffizi as fairly manageable, especially compared to the Louvre—its thirteen kilometres of galleries would take a long time to traverse even if you didn't stop for the art—but it can still be overwhelming to take in the entire Uffizi on a single visit. I like to focus on a theme, such as the Annunciation. I start with Simone

Martini's *Annunciation* in the Sienese room. Even though I find Mary's distressed, almost repulsed, expression as she reacts to the news of the Immaculate Conception rather disturbing, the extensive use of gold leaf is so beautiful, the colours so intense, the 'architecture' of the frame of pointed arches so fitting. It's my point of reference for considering the other *Annunciations*. In the hands of later painters, Mary seems more accepting of the news, and she eventually 'emerges' from the structure of arches and columns (where she is usually sitting when Gabriel finds her), with only the canvas's edge to contain the scene.

By the time I get to the other side of the 'U', the visit is no longer the casual one I had intended; a propensity to be absorbed by details means I usually surpass my ninety-minute-maximum-rule for museums (good in theory but rarely practical). I like to pause before the *Tondo Doni*, Michelangelo's round painting of the Holy Family, which is still graced by the frame that he designed for it himself—to see the strong yellows, golds and blues, the sense of movement conveyed by his seemingly sculpted figures, how Joseph is holding Jesus for the first time in the history of art. This work is also unique because it's Florence's only painting by Michelangelo.

I will always remember the first time I saw Artemisia Gentileschi's immense bloody painting of *Judith Slaying Holofernes* in the west wing. (It's now moved downstairs near the Caravaggios, but it's impossible to know where it will be once the museum is reorganised.) I had just attended a talk by the author of a novel about Artemisia's struggle as a rare seventeenth-century female artist, and having this knowledge made the discovery seem even more meaningful. The glossy oversized postcard I chose as my memento of that particular visit to the Uffizi still recalls the many memories linked with the painting: hearing the author's personal story of writing the book, reading her novel about the artist, and then the research this introduction to Artemisia has inspired.

I have returned to my place on the ledge that runs around the Loggia dei Lanzi. Leafing through my journal, I come across some notes from last summer, when I discovered artist Jean Michel Folon. The first place I saw his work was in Palazzo Vecchio's Sala d'Arme, but there were several other installations of his retrospective on display throughout the city that summer, even extending to other towns outside of Florence in order to cover the range of media the Belgian artist explored. The Forte di Belvedere hosted the largest and most impressive selection of Folon's pieces, so I made the climb up the hill often, feeling as if I were getting to know the artist a little more each time. I bought a DVD of the interview in which Folon talks about his work, falling in love with his mix of humility, honesty, enthusiasm and positive energy. It was inspiring to see how he evolved over the decades ... his desire to work in new media, the themes he developed. Like me, he felt very much at home in Florence, and I can only imagine how satisfying it must have been for him to see his work exhibited against the backdrop of the city.

I remember an evening towards the end of the exhibition, in the early days of October, as the Tuscan light became warmer and the shadows softer and longer. The park around the fort's Palazzetto allowed a full appreciation of his sculptures, and the hazy sunset skies seemed to mimic the way in which Folon's watercolours seep into one another; the shadows of people on the brick in turn reminded me of the simplified figures of Folon's bronzes.

After focusing on painting for so many years, it apparently took Folon a while to learn to design in a three-dimensional medium, but his sculpture is wonderful: *Evasion* allowed you to look through the hollow bronze 'suitcase', which framed the city; the figure of *Qualqu'un* had acquired a coat of vivid powdery rust that echoed the terracotta colour of the city's rooftops and the reddish brick of the fort's ramparts. His *Pensées*—fifteen thoughts symbolised—were fascinating. Each body, topped by a different head—a book, a cat, a suitcase, a guitar, a spool of thread—made me think of how we might use symbols to represent ourselves.

Inside the Palazzetto was an exhibit inspired by one of Folon's sculptures of his prototype man with the hat, which sits in the Northern Sea. A copy of this bronze man sat on a pile of sand in the middle of the room, and the wall-sized photographs conveyed a sense of how the original 'lives' in its setting at the sea; as the tide comes and goes, it alternately covers or reveals the figure. Upstairs, where watercolours and smaller bronzes were on display, the small windows cut out of the temporary exhibition walls allowed glimpses through the building's much larger, permanent windows, each small rectangle echoing the pictures on the walls: the views became part of the show.

Folon explored the theme of travel and produced a body of work that focused on ships. One of the ships is on an incline, but the others are all perfectly horizontal: why does it diverge this one time? There were also small boxes, with tiny ships on the inside of the lids: yet another three-dimensional way of expressing his ship theme. A corrugated cardboard 'hull' gave me the idea of using this texture to represent Florence's rooftops in my collages. I like the concept of transforming art into something new—how the subject, colours, texture or composition of a piece of art can inspire another, often completely different, creative project. A detail from a building becomes the feature of my personalised stationery, a statue comes to life in a bedtime story for my daughter, the colours from a painting inspire me to breathe new energy into my home.

Just eighteen days after this *mostra* closed—touted as the 'exhibit of a lifetime'—Folon passed away. How lucky I feel to have seen his work here, to have gained from his wisdom the confidence that, with time, I too will continue to grow as an artist.

Along the north side of Palazzo Vecchio, Via dei Gondi links Piazza della Signoria with Piazza San Firenze, sloping down slightly to follow the form of the Roman amphitheatre that once stood on this site. Flanking Via del Proconsolo, the main road that leads into the triangular piazza from the north, are two buildings that were important in Dante's time: Palazzo del Bargello and the Badia Fiorentina, which formed the civic and religious heart of a town we would barely recognise now.

In Piazza San Firenze, buildings from a range of architectural periods exist side by side. There is the stately Renaissance Palazzo Gondi, where a florist has created an oasis, complete with a splashing fountain, in the pleasant courtyard. Commanding attention opposite the florist is a Baroque façade that unifies and conceals behind it a church and the courts of law that took over a former convent and oratory.

My visiting friends always enjoy popping around the corner to check out the typical Florentine paper products at Signum, while their children prefer chasing one another up and down the steps in front of the Tribunal. I like to consider the view, with the towers of the Badia and Bargello, the one balancing the other. On the left, the Badia's bell tower emerges from a Benedictine abbey founded by Willa, the wife of the Margrave of Tuscany, in 978. Visiting hours are next to non-existent; consequently most of what I know of it is through Robert Hellenga's novel *The Sixteen Pleasures*, which is set during the period when Florence was getting back on its feet after the 1966 flood. Like many buildings, the Badia suffered severe damage, and the book describes the delicate task of saving some of its frescoes from disintegrating.

Opposite the Badia lies the thirteenth-century Bargello, whose name recalls the period in the sixteenth century when the Chief of Police, or *Bargello*, worked here. The crenellated tower and roof profile are similar to that of Palazzo Vecchio, only on a considerably smaller scale. Originally the *popolo* installed their leader, the *Capitano del Popolo*, in the palace, and later the *Podestà*.

Since the mid-1860s, when Florence became the capital of Italy, the building's lofty rooms have been used for an extensive collection of sculpture and decorative arts known as the Museo Nazionale del Bargello. I still remember the first time I came across Michelangelo's studies for his sculptures in the New Sacristy, and noticed that the unusual curve on which the figures of *Night*, *Day*, *Dusk* and *Dawn* lie seemed similar to the ones used to support Ponte Santa Trìnita. Further research led to the discovery that Michelangelo had collaborated with Ammannati on the bridge—just one more instance of this theme of interconnection I often come across as I explore Florence's history ... an endlessly fascinating process.

The courtyard, where prisoners were tortured until the 1780s, is one of the loveliest in Florence. When the death penalty was abolished by order of Grand Duke Pietro Leopoldo in 1786, the instruments of torture were burned in the very spot they were used, putting an end to the gloomy pall of torture and execution. This

The Piazzas of Florence

anniversary is now celebrated as the Festa della Toscana on the last day of November; many schools close for the day, and Tuscan cities organise events that promote solidarity and peace.

Complaining about Florence's constant renovation work—annoying and unattractive though it may be—has always seemed unnecessary in a city so full of treasures, but Piazza della Signoria's usual charm was undeniably absent between 2003 and 2005, when the *palazzo* and loggia were both obscured by scaffolding. After seeing an aerial photo from the 1980s, showing the square dug up for archaeological excavations of the old Roman town below, I knew I would have formed a very different impression of the city if this important piazza had been dismantled and barely accessible the first time I visited. It is wonderful to have the freedom to traverse the entire square in all directions, and to have nine different points of access to choose from.

As you approach Piazza della Signoria from one of the streets leading into it, music often swirls through the square, either played by the usual street musicians or as part of one of the many organised events. Tonight, on a stage set before the Loggia dei Lanzi, a Gala of Dance is showcasing a diverse program featuring a wide range of music. With the breeze fluttering their elegant understated costumes, the dancers' charisma captivates the audience for ninety minutes. After a haunting Catalan number accompanied by music from Maria del Mar Bonet, a modern piece choreographed by Lucinda Childs begins to the beat of a drum. One at a time, more instruments enter the mix, each adding more intensity and energy, until the piazza resonates with the momentum of sound and movement. In this spirit of adding layers, I think of how the new memories that transpire within the boundaries of this piazza have been layered over the old to form an ever richer story. And stretching back through a past that has been handed down from one generation to another, this piazza now holds a part of my personal history too.

# Piazza di Santa Maria Novella

I did not much care for Piazza Santa Maria Novella on my first visit. Under an overcast sky and with several buildings concealed by unsightly scaffolding, the piazza seemed dingy—nothing like it must have been when the square sat among the fields where John Ruskin once retreated for contemplation, or where Henry James lived so contentedly as he worked on his novel Roderick Hudson and W.D. Howells stayed while he did the research for Indian Summer. The church interior felt cold and gloomy, and the dull light kept the stained glass windows from showing off. A mediocre meal eaten on the patio of a touristy restaurant didn't help my first impression either.

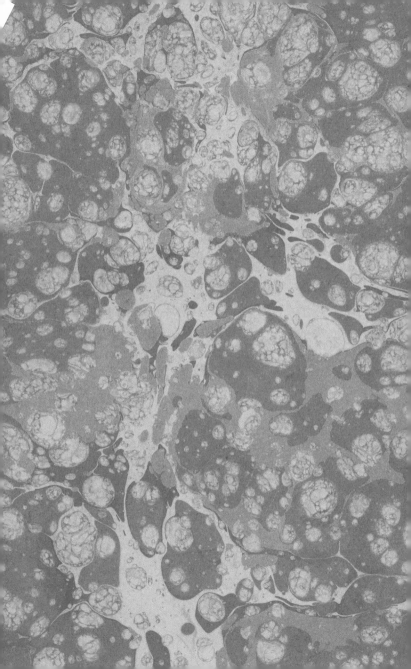

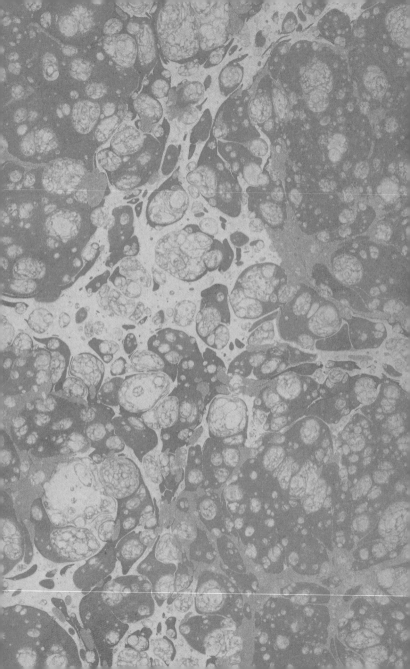

The next time I recorded a visit to Santa Maria Novella was during Ella's first trip to Florence. We were staying up in the hills near Fiesole, at the Pensione Bencistà, and I still remember the frustrating walk from the bus stop once we had arrived in *Centro*. Ella was starving—and consequently very cranky—as I pushed her, wailing in the stroller, through the streets. Once we arrived in the piazza, Ella calmed down and finally ate a sandwich on the quieter side of the steps in front of the church. The moment her hunger had been satisfied she ran off, circling through the grass with her arms spread out in imitation of the birds, delighting in scaring the pigeons away—a two-year-old's idea of power.

That day I finally saw the beautiful light coming through the stained glass of the church interior, and the new memories gave me a stronger connection to this piazza. I'm interested in just how many factors can affect one's attitude towards a place. There are personal circumstances, like the disposition of your travelling companions, or a disappointing incident, such as losing your camera or having your purse stolen. And then there's the whole 'public' mood. It can make such a big difference if a fair or market or public concert is in progress, if the sun is shining, if the place is too lifeless—or too crowded. On my first visit to Rome I headed straight for Piazza Navona—I could hardly wait to see this square I had heard so much about—but I was disappointed that the piazza was literally obscured by a *festa* for Epiphany. Yet, another time I would probably have been excited to stumble upon such an exciting celebration.

When we walk through Piazza Santa Maria Novella now, usually in transit—on our way to the station to catch a train or bus, returning home at the end of a trip, or to meet visiting friends and family—I often think of the turning-point visit with my daughter. Ella still likes to chase the pigeons whenever she has the chance, and now she's the one holding the hands of our younger visitors as they run about scaring the birds.

The mendicant orders began settling in Florence during the first half of the thirteenth century. These friars differed from the traditional cloistered monks, who retreated from the rest of the world and supported themselves through their investments in property and business. Instead, the mendicants accepted alms in order to maintain their oath of poverty, and their primary goal was to pass on their beliefs to the public; many of Florence's great piazzas were first conceived as spaces for preaching their message of faith.

The Dominicans, who promoted the teachings of the Spaniard Domingo de Guzman, were one such mendicant order. In 1221, the year of Domingo's death, the Dominicans established themselves in Florence, and were given the modest church of Santa Maria delle Vigne, named for its location among the vineyards outside the city walls.

In keeping with their different philosophies, the various mendicant orders typically set up their churches on opposite sides of the city, so while the Dominican Santa Maria Novella gives its name to the west side of Florence, the Franciscan Santa Croce lends its name to the east side. Santa Maria Novella contrasts noticeably with the church of Santa Croce, and it's interesting to discover some of the reasons behind this. While both the Dominicans and the Franciscans were defined by a belief in poverty and humility, as well as a desire to popularise religion by involving the laity, there seem to be just as many differences as similarities between the two orders.

Most importantly, the Dominicans, whose name comes from the Latin *domini canes*, 'hounds of the Lord', have a reputation for being dogmatic, while the Franciscan friars are more accepting of human infallibility. Consequently, the aristocratic neighbourhood that grew up around Santa Maria Novella reflected the intellectual foundation of the Dominican order, whereas the Franciscan *quartiere* attracted the working class, the city's artisans. The beliefs of each order naturally manifested themselves in the form of very different churches and different ways of decorating them: the Dominican churches featured rigid dogmatic fresco cycles, whereas the Franciscans favoured simpler narrative cycles.

The original Dominican church of Santa Maria Novella was much smaller, with an orientation perpendicular to the present one and facing what was once called Piazza Vecchia di Santa Maria Novella (today Piazza dell'Unità Italiana). When the Dominicans decided to build a larger church in the 1270s, the old church then became the transept of a new nave that ran north–south, and a large outdoor space in front of its façade was marked out for preaching— today's Piazza Santa Maria Novella.

The visitor entrance is no longer through the front façade, but instead via the old cemetery, which is located in a tree-filled courtyard alongside the church. Having to wait to pay the small admission fee detracts somewhat from the spontaneity of popping into the church, but one benefit is that it's now kept open all day long. Masaccio's restored *Trinity* greets visitors as they enter through the side door; just one of many notable works at this complex, it's among the earlier frescoes made using Brunelleschi's newly created rules of perspective.

On sunny days the sun filters through the church's stained glass windows, casting a rosy glow throughout the spacious nave. Despite a restoration by Vasari in the mid-sixteenth century, and the

Gothic Revival-style alterations made three hundred years later in an attempt to restore its medieval character, the spatial integrity of the church has remained intact. Six cross-vaulted bays, echoed on a smaller scale along the aisles, diminish progressively in width and change form—from a round arch to a pointed one—as they recede towards the main altar, fooling the eye into thinking the church is even longer. The sense of space created by the soaring vaults is completely different to what you experience upon entering the Franciscan realm of Santa Croce, where the wooden-trussed ceiling is darker and heavier, although it too reaches a lofty height.

Like the other major religious complexes in Florence, Santa Maria Novella contains the work of many generations of artists and has been subjected to a number of renovations and changes due to popular taste. Domenico Ghirlandaio orchestrated the great fresco cycles in the choir behind the main altar; the setting, decoration and costumes offer a treasury of information on Florentine life at the end of the fifteenth century. Ghirlandaio set the scenes of the *Life of the Virgin* and the *Life of John the Baptist*, which are alive with movement, colour and joy, against elaborately frescoed architecture.

To the right of the choir, the Cappella Strozzi di Palazzo conveys a very different feeling. Filippino Lippi's frescoed architecture leaps out at the viewer, creating a beautiful space, but the faces of the people are grey and intent—some look almost confused, others distressingly sad. There is an almost sinister sense of tension not usually felt in either his work or that of his contemporaries. These contorted human forms and expressions seem to hint at the Mannerist style to come, when painting, sculpture and architecture would break free from the rational lines of classically influenced Renaissance designs, showing a previously unseen level of emotion.

The rest of the vast complex can be accessed via a separate entrance to the left of the church: there are several cloisters, the

Cappella degli Spagnoli, the great refectory. The same bird song that echoes through all the cloisters—or any spot that hasn't been paved in this city—fills the refuge of the Chiostro Verde. Tiny daisies dot the quadrants of grass, and a quartet of cypresses grows near the old well, with their trunks and branches in varying stages of growth and states of health. Trees have always seemed to me to have a personality: the upright nature of cypresses especially reminds me of the human figure. Much like the 'after' picture of a group of people you might assemble for comparison decades later, the cypresses here have fared so differently: one is tall and robust, while two are of average height and fullness, and an unhealthy one has finally been cut to the ground.

Another part of the convent is devoted to the Farmacia e Profumeria di Santa Maria Novella. The public can enter a series of prettily decorated rooms from Via della Scala and spend some time browsing in the shop, which is perfumed by the centuries-old recipes created by the Dominican monks.

Since I first started coming to Florence, I have been collecting books written by the city's past and present visitors; these accounts have often inspired my own writing. I especially enjoy reading how other travellers have responded to the writings of those before them. A classic text about Florence that has stimulated much debate is John Ruskin's *Mornings in Florence*. According to the nineteenth-century art critic, whether or not you have the ability to 'see' Florence is determined by whether you are 'pleased' by two of Giotto's frescoes in the Chiostri dei Morti, which is situated to the north of the Chiostro Verde.

When I visit Santa Maria Novella, I can't help but think of Henry James's experience of reading Ruskin. James visited Florence several times, often for extended periods, and transformed his experiences into novels and collections of travel essays. In *Italian Hours* he describes how he picked up a copy of Ruskin's *Mornings in Florence* as he waited for a friend in Santa Maria Novella church one day. He tried to bring himself to agree with the respected critic's unflattering observations of the city, but soon grew impatient with Ruskin's intolerance of the 'new' art and architecture superimposed over the 'old', and found he was inclined to finally put the volume aside so he could enjoy the church, even if it proved—according to Ruskin—that he must be quite ignorant.

> *I had taken great pleasure in certain frescoes by Ghirlandaio in the choir of that very church; but it appeared from one of the little books that these frescoes were as naught ...*
>
> *... Then at last my friend arrived and we passed together out of the church and, through the first cloister beside it, into a smaller enclosure where we stood a while to look at the tomb of the Marchesa Strozzi-Ridolfi, upon which the great Giotto has painted four superb little pictures ... I drew forth one of my little books again, for I had observed that Mr. Ruskin spoke of them. Hereupon I recovered my tolerance; for what could be better in this case, I asked myself, than Mr. Ruskin's remarks? They are in fact excellent and charming—full of appreciation of the deep and simple beauty of the great painter's work ... One of the frescoes—it is a picture of the birth of the Virgin—contains a figure coming through a door. 'Of ornament,' I quote, 'there is only the entirely simple outline of the vase which the servant carries; of colour two or three masses of sober red and pure white, with brown and grey. That is all,' Mr. Ruskin continues. 'And if you are pleased with this you can see Florence. But if not, by all means amuse yourself there, if you find it amusing, as long as you like; you can never see it.' You can never see it.*

*This seemed to my friend insufferable ... We agreed afterwards, when in*
*a more convenient place I read aloud a good many more passages from*
*the precious tracts, that there are a great many ways of seeing Florence,*
*as there are of seeing most beautiful and interesting things, and that it is*
*very dry and pedantic to say that the happy vision depends upon our*
*squaring our toes with a certain particular chalk-mark.*

Henry James was not the only one to express indignation
about Ruskin's limited views on appreciating art; E.V. Lucas was also
compelled to note his irritation in *A Wanderer in Florence*. Lucas agrees
that the Giottos are 'very simple and telling, and I advise everyone
to open the "Mornings in Florence" and learn how the willful magic
pen deals with them; but it would be a pity to give up Ghirlandaio
because Giotto was so different, as Ruskin wished. Room for both.'
In *The City of Florence*, R.W.B. Lewis clearly takes Henry James's
side, excusing him for losing 'patience with the view that there is
rigid truth and unforgivable error in the human response to works
of art; with the "apocalyptic terminology" that suggests a kind of
damnation in not seeing things correctly; with the total absence of
any portion of *joy* in the aesthetic experience.'

It's interesting to reflect upon the remarks about Ruskin, to
consider each writer's opinion and to think about what influences
and informs our judgment and how it can change. A critic like
Ruskin was of course responding to Florence in accordance
with his education and training—but even the critical assessment
of art evolves over time. The celebrated Botticelli was only
'rediscovered' by the Pre-Raphaelites in the nineteenth century, after
having been forgotten for several centuries (and much praised by
Ruskin himself).

I have looked for Giotto's frescoes, the ones that Ruskin says
are so important. Alas, I have not yet figured out if I can really

'understand' Florence, because for some time a 'closed for restoration' sign has been hung before the blocked-off passage leading to the frescoes. You can see into the other side of the Chiostro dei Morti from the tourist office in Piazza della Stazione, but the gate is always locked. This is so indicative of the state of things in Italy: you look for something and find it's being restored (or closed for another, unknown reason). Yet, more often than not, I am rewarded with a new discovery instead.

Indeed, today it's not long before I find something intriguing. In the vaulted room once used as the great refectory, where a collection of religious objects is now displayed, it takes me a moment to register that the fresco on the end wall is actually composed of parts of two different paintings. The top half of one painting joins with the lower section of another, and the merging of the frescoed architectural features by each painter (who worked a century apart) is just ever so slightly off-centre from one another, creating a startling effect as the odd juxtaposition reveals itself after a few moments of study.

I return to the piazza, which is very popular on this gorgeous summery day. After weeks of grey skies, the sun is casting the square in its best light, and the benches are full of sun-seekers. Observing the activity offers a clue as to why most of Florence's piazzas consist of hard, unforgiving stone: signs warning people to stay off the grass do not deter teenagers from kicking around soccer balls, or sunbathers from sprawling on the remaining healthy grass. Pedestrians have worn their own paths, further contributing to the sometimes run-down feeling of this piazza. It reminds me of one of those basic architectural landscaping rules: design paths with the user in mind or they will go unused as people create their own. This is one reason why I believe that time is sometimes the best architect: a preconceived plan often lacks the knowledge needed to plan for the future.

Stone paths crisscross the piazza's grassy areas, creating a geometrical echo of the elaborate marble-patterned church façade. Marble obelisks, supported by bronze turtles, still mark either end, reminders of an annual carriage race that took place here for three hundred years. Cypress trees poking up from the church's cloisters repeat the vertical silhouette of the obelisks and bell tower, and a single gurgle emerges from a low pool at the centre of the piazza. I appreciate how Florence's fountains tend to be well proportioned and modestly decorated, perfectly attuned to the Florentine sense of restraint. While they can't compete with the fanciful Baroque ones of Rome, their simplicity is lovely.

Santa Maria Novella's façade overlooks the square from the northern end. I find it to be the most beautiful of Florence's marble church façades, perhaps because it was executed during a period of patient refinement that will probably never be repeated, but some of the appeal may lie in the patina that only time and the elements can render. The volutes are gorgeous, with an intricacy of detail that matches the rest of the façade. While the façades were not necessarily seen as integral to a church's design, and were often added later, or not at all, the timeline of this church façade corresponded more closely with that of the interior. It was mostly finished in the sixteenth century, when Leon Battista Alberti complemented the Romanesque lower section of the church façade with a harmonious upper half.

The piazza's other main feature sits opposite the church: a loggia fronting the former Ospedale di San Paolo, which recalls Brunelleschi's graceful one for the Ospedale degli Innocenti in Piazza Santissima Annunziata. At one end a glazed terracotta lunette created by Luca della Robbia celebrates the first meeting of Saint Dominic and Saint Francis. The recent opening of the Museo Nazionale Alinari della Fotografia in the building behind the loggia allows visitors to follow Piazza Santa Maria Novella's changes throughout the history of photography, as well as to see striking compositions of the city's monuments and moments.

First-floor balconies overlook the piazza from many of the *palazzi*. They must have offered a perfect place for watching the *spettacoli* in the days when festivals, tournaments and celebrations took place here. Events such as these are no longer held in Piazza Santa Maria Novella, but a week-long Scottish Market sets up in December, and each summer the parade that precedes the three annual *calcio in costume* matches leaves Santa Maria Novella before traversing the town to Piazza Santa Croce.

Who knows what the future holds for Piazza Santa Maria Novella. For the past couple of years the city has been implementing a complete makeover of this piazza, and the first stage of the project has recently concluded with the restoration of the two obelisks and the loggia at the southern end. The most intense phase is currently in progress; for several months the gorgeous church façade has been bandaged with a shroud of gauzy fabric that hides the scaffolding, and the centre of the piazza has been turned into a construction site, the stone paving completely torn up.

I look forward to the day when the many towers of scaffolding around Piazza Santa Maria Novella will finally all be removed, revealing the unfettered version of the square seen in paintings and drawings from times past. The entire area will be freshly paved with new stone, its hard edges tempered by herb borders. Living through this renewal of Piazza Santa Maria Novella seems to be tempering my memories of the square too. For now, I look beyond the chaos of the renovation, awaiting not only the piazza's metamorphosis, but also that of my sentiments towards it.

# Piazza di Santa Croce

Over seven hundred years ago, the Franciscans created Piazza Santa Croce as a space where they could preach outdoors, and thus draw more citizens to their teachings. To this day the church of Santa Croce and its piazza have held together this neighbourhood, which takes the same name. As one of the most expansive squares in the city, it still hosts many civic events, from fairs and markets to protests and sports events. Made up of a crisp geometrical arrangement of white, rose and green marbles, the church's façade makes a colourful backdrop for this piazza that serves as a sort of big front yard for the residents and tourists.

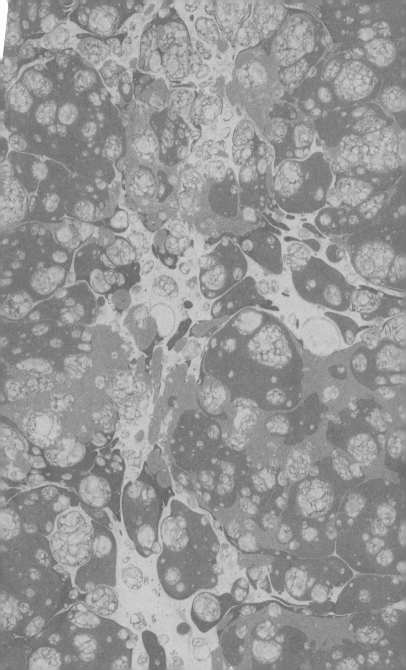

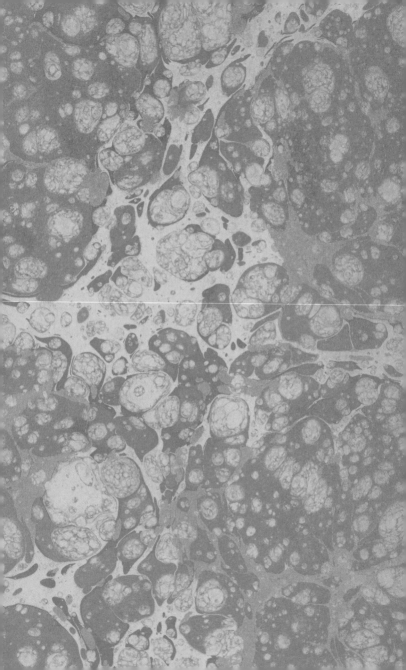

From my spot on a bench in the square I can see Palazzo dell'Antella, which records several historical notes on its front wall. A seven-metre marker from the 1966 flood reminds people of its devastating magnitude, while a plaque, dated 1565, has indicated the centre line for several centuries of sporting events. Above the door sits a bust of Grand Duke Cosimo II, and the entire façade is decorated with a fresco program celebrating this fourth grand duke—the result of a twenty-day painting frenzy commissioned by former owner Niccolo dell'Antella in the seventeenth century.

The important Piccolomini family from Siena acquired Palazzo dell'Antella through marriage in the last century, and now they rent out a number of upmarket apartments with views onto the piazza. Today I see a couple of boys leaning out of the window, watching the scene below—teenagers passing around a soccer ball, children racing around on their bikes, elderly men chatting, tour groups disintegrating in the huge space.

Writer R.W.B. Lewis and his wife lived in Palazzo dell'Antella for six months in the early 1990s, and in *The City of Florence* Lewis wrote fondly about their routine and the many events they witnessed in Piazza Santa Croce during this time. I enjoy reading the minutiae of his daily four-minute walk from the palazzo to the news stand on the other side of the piazza (which still sells the dailies), hearing how much he delighted in the historical details that were part of every outing. Lewis acknowledged the many criticisms of Santa Croce's nineteenth-century façade (too sterile, too modern, too boring), but believed that 'one can—after living near it and looking at it day after day—develop a certain affection for it. We could not resist telling each other, about the church, that we'd grown accustomed to her facade, it almost made the day begin.'

Behind Santa Croce's pristine neo-Gothic façade lies the basilica and its rich complex of cloisters and museums. The Franciscans had hoped to exceed the dimensions of the Dominican church of Santa Maria Novella when they commissioned the present structure to replace the original in 1294, and the church is certainly an impressively large and serene space. Arnolfo di Cambio, who was in charge of several of the city's major projects in the 1290s, is attributed as the designer, and indeed, he succeeded in outdoing the Dominicans: Santa Croce's dimensions are second only to Florence's Duomo, and it is the largest Franciscan basilica in Italy.

This competitive spirit about the church's size may not seem in keeping with the Franciscans' philosophy—and in fact, at the time, there was quite a debate about its proposed grandness. In the end, their faith that they would need a large church to accommodate all the believers they hoped to attract won out. The city sponsored the project, which was built on an Egyptian cross plan, a 'T' in shape. Several wealthy families stepped in with commissions for the chapels flanking the main altar, and paid for their decoration as well; soon the entire church was covered with frescoes. But in the sixteenth century Vasari implemented a program of immense wall chapels and monuments for Florence's deceased greats, and all of the frescoes were whitewashed.

As was common throughout Florence's history of churches, the façade was not added until many centuries later. In old drawings and a few early photos, we can see how the unfinished exterior looked before it was built in the mid-nineteenth century—similar to how the churches of San Lorenzo and Santa Maria del Carmine remain to this day, and as the Duomo appeared until the late 1870s. The varied marble façades are more distinctive, easier to recognise, but I do admire the honesty of the bare stone ones. I can't help but think of the false fronts that characterised the saloons and general stores of the Wild West, of a natural tendency to augment, to exaggerate the true size of buildings, making them look taller and more impressive than they were—much like the strip malls and suburban developments that are so popular today.

While the church of Santa Maria Novella is airy and spacious, I prefer Santa Croce's interior; it reminds me of a huge covered outdoor room, with a piazza-like quality. Under the wooden-beamed ceiling—which John Ruskin rather unkindly compared to that of a barn—are altars, cenotaphs and plaques, and more than two hundred and seventy other tombs pave a large portion of the floor. The aisles, defined by pointed arches, are lined with tombs commemorating some of the city's most celebrated men, whose legacy covers an impressive range of the arts, sciences and humanities: Leonardo Bruni, Michelangelo, Galileo, Dante, Machiavelli.

The Bardi and Peruzzi family chapels contain the remaining portions of Giotto's groundbreaking frescoes of the lives of Saint Francis, Saint John the Baptist and Saint John the Evangelist. In the first decades of the fourteenth century, Giotto heralded a new trend in religious art, giving emotion to what had been up to that time merely iconic figures. Nature served as both his teacher and his source of inspiration and, as a result, his work conveyed a humanness not previously seen in the portrayal of religious stories. He seems a fitting artist to have illustrated the teachings of Saint Francis, whose order was founded upon love and an acceptance of humanity. In keeping with the theme of compassion and goodwill, the church is filled with donation boxes for just about any cause you might wish to contribute to: *'Offerti per i poveri'*, offers for the poor; *'in onore della Madonna'*, in honour of the Virgin Mary; *'caritas'*, charity; *'per i restauri della chiesa*', for the restoration of the church; *'per i fratelli bisognosi'*, for the needy brothers.

As I look at the sign with the floor plan and notes about the church, I like to listen to the comments of other visitors. 'What a beautiful ceiling!' says a woman to her companion, happily unaware of Ruskin's negative opinion of it. 'I see the Medici influence extended all the way to Santa Croce,' observes one woman when she notices the Medici Chapel near to the sacristy. 'Come on! We have all of this to see!' says a young man to his friend, and I sense the friend's reluctance to rush the visit just so he can check this church off the list. There is a lot of ground to cover here ...

After wandering through the basilica for a little while, I exit into the First Cloister, where cypress trees commemorating men who died in World War I sway in a patch of grass. Cloisters typically share the same basic symmetrical design—a covered loggia runs along the perimeter of a geometric garden, which is open to the sky—but this cloister is very different from the others: it is an 'L' shape instead of a rectangle, and the continuous arcade, broken by other architectural features, incorporates various levels.

Along an upper loggia flanking the basilica is a new exhibit showing several of the proposals that were made for the façade. A section at the end of the corridor has been partitioned off to provide an art studio, where wooden models, paintings and works in terracotta are currently in progress. As I stand in this bright and spacious loggia overlooking the cloister, thinking how amazing a space this must be for the artists to work in, I overhear singing coming from somewhere below.

The voices draw me down to the Cappello dei Pazzi, which lies off the ground level of the First Cloister. While it is large for a chapel, the size is modest for a building. The manageable scale allowed Brunelleschi to interpret his architectural ideals in a highly detailed and controlled fashion: this chapel is considered his masterpiece. The space is perfect for the voices of the twenty-five young singers, who stand under the dome, wearing flip-flops and T-shirts, spiked hair and ponytails, and sounding like modern day angels. The impromptu audience fills the benches that line the walls (where the brothers and the religious community used to sit for their chapter meetings), feeling the magic in this melding of music and architecture, both in harmony.

Once the choir has finished singing its impressive repertoire, I return to the cloister to find that the leader has switched to the role of tour guide—and I remember how much I would still like to see in this complex today. Next to the Pazzi Chapel, down in the Chiostro Antico (worth seeing to compare this earlier one with the Renaissance cloisters) is a museum dedicated to Pietro Parigi. From the early twentieth century, this artist designed striking stamps for lithographs that graced books, periodicals and posters, and in which many of Florence's buildings appear. A sampling of Parigi's original stamps lie in cases too, some of them impressively large. The bold shapes and lines that are typical of this technique seem to invite creativity; I imagine hand-printing a dozen of my favourites, then using different media and techniques to give them life and colour.

At the other end of the cloister is the Museo dell'Opera di Santa Croce, which displays a collection of items related to the church. Cimabue's damaged *Crucifix*, another reminder of the 1966 flood, hangs in the refectory. Being so close to the river, the low-lying Santa Croce district suffered some of the worst damage, but there was a silver lining—the area experienced a revitalisation. This is where the *ciompi*, Florence's poorer working class, had lived for centuries under the protection of the Franciscans, and it was in dire need of attention.

The serene Second Cloister is tucked further into the complex, beyond the first. A loggia wraps around this simple space, graced by an old well at its centre, and rose bushes are clustered in each quarter of the geometrical lawn. Brunelleschi gave this cloister good bones, although sun and rain and time have worn away parts of the columns, leaving their capitals half disintegrated, and the designs of the stone roundels between the arches have lost much of their relief. But the grass is trimmed, the roses pruned, the well transformed into a handsome container for plants.

The shadows of the loggia's arches move slowly across the wall, marking the passing hours. How peaceful it is here. There are only the voices of the visitors enjoying the sun—and the noisy birds, who seem to be trying to drown out the various conversations. The ledges that run between the columns offer places to sit—or lie, as one woman is doing. In most cloisters, a guard will be quick to admonish you if your feet leave the ground, but there's more freedom here: you can also walk up to the middle of the garden and sit on the steps at the well's base. Another example of Florence's tendency towards simple focal points, the well features spare but elegant wrought-iron curves gathered together and topped by a cross. At the leather school behind the church, there's a great old photograph of a former class gathered in the cloister, with one maverick balancing at the very top of the well.

I often leave the complex via the leather school, which leads around the back of the church's main altar. The Franciscans and the Gori and Casini families, who had been leather artisans since the

1930s, created the Scuola del Cuoio so that World War II orphans could have a chance to learn a practical trade. The Franciscan brothers converted an old dormitory for the students; their workbenches were placed in the corridor, where today's artisans also have their workstations. Visitors can watch them applying the finishing touches to desk sets, jewellery cases and albums, or wander through the former cells looking for leather bags, jackets and wallets. And today the school also teaches their techniques to a wider audience.

The Medici coat of arms that adorns the leather school reminds us that the family had other connection to Santa Croce besides their chapel near the main basilica. The Medici had donated the dormitory to the Franciscans back in the fifteenth century, and then commissioned Ghirlandaio's workshop to fresco its walls. Their familiar coat of arms, which featured a varying number of *palle*, 'balls', over time, appears throughout Florence.

From Piazza Santa Croce you can follow the perimeter of the former Roman Amphitheatre, whose outline clearly remains in the curve of the street and the buildings that conform to it. This is where spectators came to watch the gladiatorial contests, the first in a long tradition of sports events held in this quarter of the city.

The piazza itself has been a long-time venue for the annual *calcio in costume*, a traditional sport played in costume. It consists of three matches played between Florence's four neighbourhoods—San Giovanni, Santa Croce, Santa Maria Novella and Santo Spirito. During the period leading up to 24 June (the feast day of San

Giovanni), Piazza Santa Croce assumes a different personality. Sand is laid over the stone paving, and the church façade is nearly obscured by the stadium seating that surrounds the temporary playing field.

The game, or at least a related version, dates back to about the fifteenth century; it resembles soccer and rugby, but also involves a large amount of wrestling. The most memorable of these historic games was played in 1530, when Florence was under siege by the imperial troops of Charles V. The Florentines boldly chose to show that, despite their situation, their spirit was still alive. (Later that year, however, starving and dejected, they capitulated.) While the *calcio in costume* tradition ceased towards the end of the seventeenth century, it was revived on the four-hundredth anniversary of that famous 1530 game.

Before each match, five hundred Florentines in historic costume march across town on their way to the piazza. The testosterone that will sustain the players is palpable as each rowdy team is cheered on past. Group by group, the procession makes its way onto the pitch, followed by the cannons that will proclaim each goal. Finally, an elderly man arrives, leading a heifer; whereas once the beast would have been slaughtered, roasted and eaten by the winning team, these days it merely serves as a symbolic prize.

One year we were swept along with the parade and ended up in the stands, where we watched the impressive flag-throwing show. The music of trumpets and drums filled the air as the musicians riled up the crowd to welcome the players onto the field. Once the game got under way, it seemed that the goal of getting the ball to their opponents' end was secondary to terrorising the enemy team; at any given time about half the players were engaged in a headlock or some other strange form of embrace, and appeared to be dancing in slow motion in what is a truly violent game.

In fact, exceptional rough housing that year, coupled with brutal violence that led to twenty-one men being admitted to hospital before the first game of the 2006 season had even started, caused officials to suspend the match while they rewrote the rules. After a quiet summer this past year, the *calcio in costume* is scheduled to bring its particular brand of excitement to Piazza Santa Croce again in 2008.

This is one of the few piazzas without a centrally placed focal point. There's a fountain at the western end, but Piazza Santa Croce's main feature is really the everyday show in the middle of the piazza. On this Sunday afternoon someone is pounding out a rhythm on a drum as teenagers play frisbee and a toddler splashes in puddles from the rain earlier. Mothers cycle past, their child seats empty today, and Asian women with scarves draped over their arms walk around beseeching potential customers; still, plenty of space remains for the numerous tour groups heading to and from the church.

Situated on the *primo piano* of a south-facing *palazzo* is a generous terrace that I recognise from paintings and drawings dating back several centuries; from there spectators would have observed the celebrations in the piazza as well as from balconies that once extended from many of the buildings. This afternoon a couple is tending the vines and overflowing planters in what is now their urban garden. They are lucky to have this space, with its semi-private position overlooking the piazza: Florence is a city without front yards, and this is probably the closest thing to resembling one in the centre. While there are countless courtyards and terraces, they only accommodate a small percentage of the population. But city Italians are accustomed to sharing space, to living more public lives—the neighbourhood piazza replaces the private outdoor space that is usually part of suburban or country homes.

Living in Florence is a very different experience from that of living in my old neighbourhood in southern California, where it was typical for neighbours to wave as they drove their cars into the driveway or garage and then walk straight into their houses. People had cocktails and barbecues in their backyards, and the front yard tended to be more for show. We used our front yard a lot though; the house was situated on a tiny street with lots of young families and had a pleasant west-facing lawn that sloped gently down to the street, so we often took picnic meals to the dappled shade of its birch trees.

Sometimes it still feels strange not to have our own garden, especially when I remember the many outdoor spaces that surrounded our house. To one side was the *porte-cochère*, a covered porch where carriages would once have dropped off their passengers. Instead of using it for the car, I planted a hydrangea garden around the little fountain and created an all-purpose room for the warm months, which struck a perfect balance between semi-public and semi-private. Then there was an almost secret place in the narrow side yard, where French doors had once led out to a tiny brick-paved patio; while it was a bit awkward to reach, this spot made a great nook for peaceful breakfasts. In the backyard I built a sandbox and put up makeshift tents for Ella; we held Easter egg hunts and hosted gatherings with friends on the lawn; and on a really hot day, the little honeysuckle- and morning glory-covered gazebo was the best place to sit with a glass of lemonade. We were lucky to have enough space to plant tomatoes and flowers and herbs as well.

In Florence, most of us have to make do with a few window boxes; I cherish my pots of herbs. I used to enjoy the nursery outing every couple of months, but then actually getting everything planted would become another nagging project to add to an already long list. Once I found time to tend to my garden's needs I always enjoyed the process—and certainly the rewards—but it seemed like endless upkeep. Now I allow the available space to limit me. I find the eight or ten herbs and occasional flowers keep me content and busy enough, and the manageable scale of my 'garden' equals less stress. A good day of gardening now consists of doing a little deadheading and pruning, topping up the soil and the biggest pleasure—harvesting for cooking or making small bouquets—and it has returned to being a pleasurable activity that takes only as much time as I choose to spend on it.

A big part of being happy seems to be just figuring out how much of something we need—and acknowledging that we each have different needs. My mother keeps a big garden in Virginia (perhaps as compensation for a decade of living in city apartments across Asia). I love how she's an inspiration to Ella, who pores over gardening books as she tries to create her own garden on paper.

I think the reason we manage so well without all of the marvellous outdoor rooms we once had is because the piazzas have taken their place. I suppose it is somewhat unusual not to long for a private garden; the dream where I come from—perhaps no longer as simple as a white picket fence surrounding the yard—definitely implies outdoor space you can call your own. I would love a tiny terrace though—just enough space for a small table and a couple of chairs, a lemon tree and more herbs. But for the moment, living across the street from the Boboli Garden is enough.

On 19 March, Piazza Santa Croce hosts a *fiera* in honour of Saint Joseph's feast day, and a huge market of everyday goods and a few ethnic and artisan stalls takes over the space. There's the *calcio in costume* in the summer, and a German Christmas market fills the square for a few weeks each December. Other events are held in between the usual annual ones, but for the most part, the piazza operates in a day-to-day capacity, hosting the residents and the vast number of visitors who have come to see Giotto's frescoes, Brunelleschi's Pazzi Chapel and Cimabue's *Crucifix*.

For me, Piazza Santa Croce holds happy memories of quick but worthwhile stops at Boccadama for a *caffè* and a slice of something sweet, or long visits to the church and time spent in my favourite cloister. More than anything else though, I think of the pleasure of finding an empty spot on a bench and watching Sunday afternoon happen in the square. How wonderful that the residents have reclaimed this piazza, which for so long was a parking lot with the huge statue of Dante rising in the middle of the sea of cars. Traffic is now banned, Dante sits on the steps in front of the church, and once again the people and their activities have taken their rightful place as Piazza Santa Croce's focal point.

# Piazza della Repubblica

Piazza della Repubblica's story is the oldest in Florence. Villanovan and Etruscan remains have been excavated in this area, and the present day piazza lies at the intersection of the two principal roads of the Roman town of Florentia: the Cardo Maximus, which ran north–south, and the Decumanus, which ran east–west. First as the Forum, then as Florence's major market from medieval times, this area has been a dynamic meeting spot and place of exchange ever since.

Despite its long and colourful history, today the square is not one of Florence's more charming piazzas—at least that's what most passionate architecture and design critics will tell you. Not everyone agrees though; despite the insensitive overhaul of the area in the late nineteenth century, the piazza's offering of cafés attracted a range of literary, artistic and political groups for several decades, and today it is popular with tourists and residents. The plant market held under the loggia each week, street artists who draw crowds daily and a cheerful carousel that fills one corner from October to May each go a long way towards restoring a sense of human scale and liveliness to this square. I've met many people who name it as their favourite. 'Oh, that's where the fun Greek quartet plays?' 'I loved sitting on Caffè Gilli's patio.'

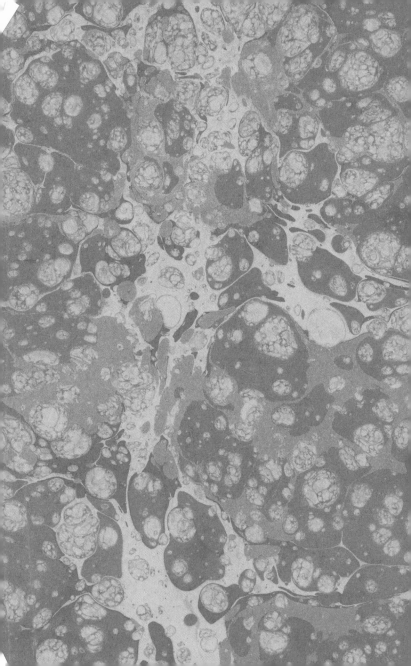

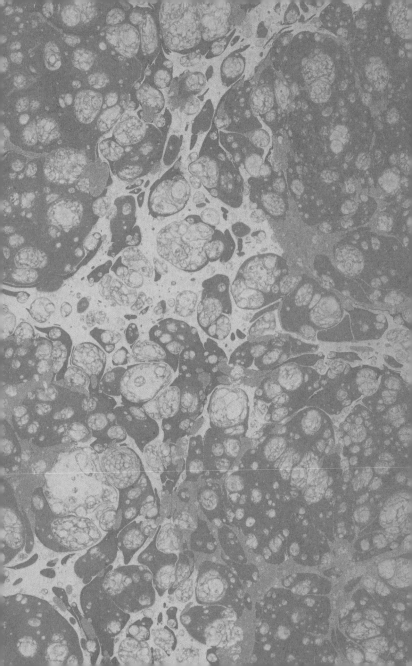

In the 1880s, a controversial urban renewal scheme was implemented in an effort to modernise the city. The project led to the disappearance of the crowded network of narrow streets and the run-down jumble of structures that had grown up around the lively Mercato Vecchio. Churches, homes, workshops, towers, loggias and piazzas—including the earlier property of the Medici family and their original parish church, San Tommaso—were sacrificed. The modern piazza that replaced the market area differed greatly from the kind of spaces created by the Franciscans and the Dominicans as venues for preaching. Instead, following the regular way in which the Romans had once laid out their Forum, it assumed the shape of a rectangle, and its monumental new buildings presented neoclassic façades, devoid of character.

During the demolition, artist Telemaco Signorini wandered around with his oil paints, capturing the quaintness of the old market area on canvas. Legend says that when one of the city engineers saw Signorini crying, he asked if the tears were for the ugliness of the buildings being torn down. Signorini responded that no, he was crying about the ugly new buildings that were going up, referring to the same ones that define the edges of the piazza now. It's true that they couldn't compete with the characterful marketplace that had developed over a period of centuries. Indeed, harmonious urban spaces seem more likely to occur when a need drives the design and the space then evolves from this need.

Because of my background in architecture, and the critical viewpoint that seems to naturally accompany it, I didn't imagine I would ever find a reason to like Piazza della Repubblica. From an architectural point of view, I still find it very unattractive—especially the over-scaled arch—but with time I have come to appreciate the appeal of the *place*. Anywhere people feel comfortable congregating becomes intrinsically interesting: human presence gives life to a space, and likewise, the most handsome buildings remain cold and emotionless if people aren't inclined to spend time there. And now this piazza has become part of my family's history. On a jet-lagged stroll through the city one November dawn, with only the street cleaners as witnesses, my brother asked his girlfriend to marry him, and later that day we all returned to the piazza for a celebratory lunch at Caffè Gilli.

For me, Piazza della Repubblica is intertwined with the concept of leisure. You could spend the better part of a day here, browsing the stores, sitting in the cafés, watching a film. My favourite day to come is Thursday, when the plant and flower market brings life to the loggia on the west side of the piazza. I look for the latest annuals and visit Francesca Neri's stand for her wide selection of herbs, browse through the selection of books at Libreria Edison, take a few minutes for a cappuccino and pastry at Gilli's elegant bar. WhenI need something for the apartment, I head to the homewares floor at La Rinascente department store, and it's always fun to check out the fashions at Zara. On the occasions when I find time to write letters to friends and family, I bring them to the central post office; there's a shop of office supplies, books, music, movies and toys to amuse customers while they wait for their numbers to be called in the grand hall (usually for ages). You never know who will serve you. Sometimes it's a surprisingly friendly person, other times an employee giving an Oscar-worthy portrayal of the stereotypical Italian government worker.

La Colonna dell'Abbondanza was set up at the centre of the marketplace in 1428. The column originally supported a statue of

*Abundance* by Donatello, as well as a bell that marked the opening and closing of the market, and debtors and other dishonest citizens were chained to it as a warning to the rest of the population. Three centuries later, another version of *Abundance*, by Giovanni Battista Foggini, replaced Donatello's after it was destroyed when the column collapsed. Nowadays elderly men, international art students and construction workers gather beneath a copy of Foggini's statue throughout the day. I like to sit on the bench at the base of this column that has marked the symbolic centre of the town for two millennia, watching the pedestrians and cyclists passing through Piazza della Repubblica. They are on their way north to the Duomo or heading south to cross Ponte Vecchio, west to Via Tornabuoni in search of the designer shops or east for any number of reasons.

Another, much smaller focal point that attracts people has appeared in Piazza della Repubblica recently—a bronze sculpture of the historic centre. People crowd around it, delighting in finding the many landmarks; already the bell towers have turned shiny from being touched. The piazzas really stand out in this three-dimensional map of the city, appearing as voids, with no signs of being the nodes of activity or 'positive' spaces they actually are. The model offers an interactive means of helping citizens and travellers to find their bearings within the city … if only it had been aligned with the northern point of the compass: the shadows on the model would have perfectly mimicked those of the city.

For several decades Piazza della Repubblica's dominant feature was an equestrian statue of King Vittorio Emanuele II, which had been placed in the centre of the piazza to commemorate Florence's stint as the capital of Italy in the 1860s. It was later moved to the entrance of Le Cascine, and the piazza's name was changed to reflect Italy's choice to be unified in a republic.

While Florence is still learning to cope with cars in streets and piazzas that were designed for pedestrians and carriages, in the last couple of decades most of the centre's piazzas-turned-parking lots have been returned to the pedestrians. Recently installed concrete spheres now keep cars from entering Piazza della Repubblica as well—with the additional benefit of inviting children to play a game of leapfrog—and the square has begun hosting works from the temporary art exhibitions that are often interspersed throughout the city's piazzas.

For the Cow Parade exhibition in 2005, a row of life-sized resin cows—each one used as a three-dimensional 'canvas' by a different artist—drew a lot of attention. My favourite featured human hands thrusting out of the cow, each presenting a resin 'hamburger'. Last summer the marble *Canta alla Vita* by sculptor Jorge Jimenez Deredia, showing four stages of a disc-shaped female form, soaked up the sun, while this year Roberto Barni's two figures clinging to opposite sides of a bronze cylinder laid on its side amuses—and confounds—visitors.

In contrast to the portraits that artists and writers painted of the piazza in times past—an utter confusion of noise, merchandise and people—the present day carousel, the hawkers showing off the latest Chinese toys, the street artists and the musicians are pretty tame entertainment. It would have been fun to witness the bustle of the old marketplace. In her novel *Romola*, George Eliot (who would have seen the Mercato Vecchio before it was torn down) leads her characters straight to the chaos of the market in the last decade of the fifteenth century—on the day of Lorenzo il Magnifico's death to be precise—and we see the piazza in its true role: as a place of exchange for not only goods, but also information, ideas and a range of human emotion.

This part of the city was also home to other markets. As long ago as 1290, there was a loggia for the trading of grain on the site of an eighth-century oratory dedicated to San Michele. A fire barely a decade later necessitated a new structure, which was destined to become a combined granary, market and oratory. The purported miracles of a painted Madonna in the loggia attracted a devoted audience, so eventually the arcades were filled in and an elaborate tabernacle was built to house the Madonna; from that point the building's role became solely religious.

The building's form and position are unusual for a Florentine church; they are typically absorbed into the urban fabric, sharing their walls with residences and shops. But Orsanmichele is freestanding, a rectangular block unto itself. Taking advantage of this feature, the seven major guilds and five minor ones were each entrusted with commissioning a statue of its patron saint, which was then placed in an exterior niche. A spirit of competition among the guilds led to the outstanding Renaissance statues encircling the church—works by Donatello, Ghiberti, Giambologna and others. For several years the only time you could visit the interior was to hear a concert given by the Orchestra da Camera Fiorentina, but Orsanmichele has recently reopened its doors to the public. Once again, the church offers a cool place to gather one's thoughts and take a break from the bustle of *Centro*, as well as the chance to see the famous tabernacle.

As far back as the eleventh century, the so-called Mercato Nuovo developed just down Via Calimala. The name, which translates to New Market, refers to the fact that the current structure wasn't built until the mid-sixteenth century. The structure became known as the straw market, for the straw goods that were then sold under the loggia, but today the *mercato* is popular with visitors looking for leather goods, linens, scarves and souvenir trinkets. Only at the end of the day, once the train of vendors' carts has begun its homeward procession, can you truly appreciate the lovely space; the ensemble of columns, which support twelve spacious cross-vaults, and the bronze *Porcellino* finally re-emerge. Rumour has it that feeding the boar a coin and rubbing his snout guarantees a return visit to Florence, so it is usually surrounded by visitors waiting in line to capture the moment on film.

Vendors had been bringing their goods to the Mercato Vecchio for centuries, and many of them stubbornly continued to set up their stalls in the neighbourhood even once the old marketplace had disappeared. Eventually they all moved to today's Mercato Centrale, a cast-iron structure built in the 1870s. Beer houses and cafés then took over the ground floors of the imposing buildings in the new piazza, which became known as Piazza Vittorio Emanuele II, in honour of Italy's first king. These cafés started drawing intellectuals and artists, and an exchange of ideas slowly began to replace the exchange of goods that had taken place in this piazza for so long.

I am treating myself to a table on Gilli's patio, sipping an exquisite cappuccino while eating the best pastry in the city—a *brioche alla crema*, filled with custard. The café's tradition of excellent pastries dates back to 1733, when a Swiss family first opened Gilli on the nearby Via dei Calzaiuoli. This is the café I tend to choose when coming to Piazza della Repubblica; I like the sunny aspect of this particular corner, and find its marble bar the most inviting.

I can't help but wonder what these historic cafés must have been like in their heyday, when political, literary and artistic figures used to meet here regularly. From all accounts they were lively spots. In 1897 the Reininghaus brothers opened a beer house in the new piazza, on the site of a wine bar left over from the days of the Mercato Vecchio. It was named after the brothers, but the Florentines had a hard time pronouncing the German name and began calling it Le Giubbe Rosse because of the waiters' red jackets. While it seems to have had a quiet start, Le Giubbe Rosse began attracting the progressive thinkers of the day, and it became the 'office' of the Futurists in 1913. This rowdy group was intent on breaking social rules and freeing up creativity, and apparently there was much arguing—and occasionally, even physical violence. While Le Giubbe Rosse experienced a decline of cultural energy after World War II, in the last couple of decades the café has begun a cultural initiative, sponsoring literary meetings and lending its walls to art exhibits. It would be amusing to hear what the no-nonsense Futurists would have to say about the colourful fleece blankets that appear on the patio chairs in winter to keep a twenty-first-century clientele comfortable.

Across the square, Paszkowski was opened by a Polish businessman. Its patrons were harder to classify—they were neither bourgeois nor working class—but apparently the politically charged groups from Le Giubbe Rosse and Gilli felt comfortable stopping in too. Before Italy became involved in World War I, Paszowski was popular with its supporters. In recent years it has gained the epithet 'Caffè Concerto', for the live orchestra that draws customers to the patio in the evenings.

When the area under Piazza della Repubblica's north-western block was excavated in the 1880s, Villanovan tombs were found preserved between layers of sand under an intact Roman pavement, and a fountain, thought to have been located in the Forum, was also discovered. Once the new buildings went up, the Gambrinus, another popular eating and meeting spot, opened here, although in later years it was reduced to a small café with a movie theatre. The cinema officially closed this summer, although 'Fifty Nights of Cinema' is currently screening there, and the theatre is likely to continue hosting similar events. Being able to pop downstairs for a coffee during the intermission feels most civilised, and in the past it wasn't uncommon for parents to send their children up to the movie while they remained in the café to chat.

It's interesting to contemplate the clientele of these cafés, and the atmosphere their discussions, beliefs and arguments must have generated. I have always liked the idea of a circle for discussion. One of the most fascinating books I have ever come across— *A Pattern Language* by Christopher Alexander and his team at the Center for Environmental Structure in Berkeley, California—could inspire endless hours of discussion. My introduction to Alexander came when I was earning my architecture degree, but it's much more than a book about architecture: facets of sociology, psychology and culture that comprise built form have been taken into consideration to create two hundred and fifty-three patterns, resulting in a specific 'language'—a language of building and, even more significantly, a language for living.

It begins with the larger patterns that define a community, such as 'Four Story Limit', which allows people to have a sense of connection to the rest of the world even when they are in their homes and offices, a connection that tends to disappear with high-rises; 'Nine Percent Parking', which limits parking to no more than nine per cent of a given area, as it destroys human scale and contact in cities; 'Small Public Squares', which highlights the importance of public outdoor rooms, and reminds us to consider the number of people who will use them so they won't be too big—and therefore go unused; and 'High Places', which emphasises our need for landmarks—and a chance to get perspective on our world.

Next Alexander moves onto patterns that should characterise individual buildings, and then includes a section on finishing the details of the building and its outdoor space. As I read through the patterns, even the names of many of them evoke appealing images, of the kinds of places where you want to curl up with your thoughts, a good book, have a nap, chat with friends, eat a celebratory meal.

The series of patterns concludes with 'Things From Your Life'—a reminder to surround ourselves with things we love, that tell our story. Of course, following a list of patterns does not ensure good design—in the first volume of the series, *A Timeless Way of Building*, Alexander spends over five hundred pages trying to define the elusive 'quality without a name' that makes for good architecture—but it's a starting point. I recognise that one reason why I so enjoy living in Florence is for its Public Outdoor Rooms, Individually Owned Shops, Street Cafés and Corner Groceries, to name a few; they all add up to create a congenial and fulfilling environment. Some day I would like to count how many of the patterns are part of my life here.

If I were ever to organise a circle of discussion at Gilli, I would invite Christopher Alexander—to hear his opinion on Florence as a place to live and to witness the tirade on Piazza della Repubblica that would surely be forthcoming. The square goes against just about everything he stands for. And yet ...

As I sit on Gilli's orderly patio, watching the well dressed people traversing the piazza with shopping bags, mobile phones pressed to

their ears, it's hard to imagine that the Ghetto once lay in the block behind us. Although the words engraved over the nineteenth-century monumental arch state that the piazza was 'rescued from squalor'—and it's true that parts, such as the abandoned former Ghetto, were badly degraded—every source I have found expresses the belief that destroying the old marketplace was a crime. Considering the controversy though, it's difficult to understand how the project was ever approved or executed. Of course there were also supporters of the cleansing movement: a journalist who went by the name of 'Jarro' wrote scandalous articles about the poor conditions of the area, which some say were exaggerated for impact, but many people couldn't help but agree with him. Fortunately, the destruction of historic buildings was halted before it went further than Piazza della Repubblica, especially since Florence had already suffered the levelling of its final circle of walls, forever changing the character of the city.

Today the names of the remaining streets still offer clues to what used to be. Via Calimala—*calimala* means 'fleece'—was once in the quarter of the foreign wool merchants, while Via Pelliceria, or 'street of the furriers', was once lined with fur sellers, and lay at the heart of the goldsmiths' quarter. The only reminder of the early Medici property is the Via de' Medici, and this is also the case for many other families; it seems that every street pays homage to the activities or citizens from Florence's history. Other traces of the past exist too—old building fragments at the Museo di Firenze Antica in the convent of San Marco; maps and paintings in the Museo di Firenze Com'era near Piazza del Duomo; photographs in the Museo Nazionale Alinari della Fotografia in Piazza Santa Maria Novella.

For me Piazza della Repubblica is most appealing at Christmas time, when the smell of roasted chestnuts fills the air. An enormous evergreen tree, covered with dozens of strings of white lights, sits in the middle, a sort of urban garden of planters improvised around it. Nearby there's a tiny structure devoted to publicising *Inverno a Firenze*, Winter in Florence, with information on the many events that fill the shortest days of the year. An impressive display of Christmas lights runs overhead along the entire length of Via dei Calzaiuoli and enters Piazza della Repubblica at Via degli Speziali. The cafés and shops get dressed up for the holidays, the carousel spins its magic for children, and the discordant oversized arch recedes among the cheer and colour.

# Piazza di Santa Trìnita

I have stopped in Piazza Santa Trìnita to readjust my bags of plants from the Thursday market in Piazza della Repubblica. It's hard to resist sitting here for a little while, watching the comings and goings from the stone bench that runs along the front of Palazzo Bartolini-Salimbeni. Vespas, buses, cars and bicycles crisscross and intersect, ringing bells and honking, and meanwhile, a number of passers-by join me along the bench.

One after the other, several young women say 'Smells like basil' as they pass me. I laugh when one of them notices the basil plant poking out of one of my bags: mystery solved. An older woman, perfectly coiffed and wearing elegant sunglasses, walks past, wheeling her bicycle with one hand and enjoying a cigarette with the other, tranquil even in the heat and traffic. Across the street, in front of the church, another woman sits cross-legged, asking everyone who passes for an offering. She seems to be at her post whenever the church is open—a small mound of pattern dwarfed by the tall façade.

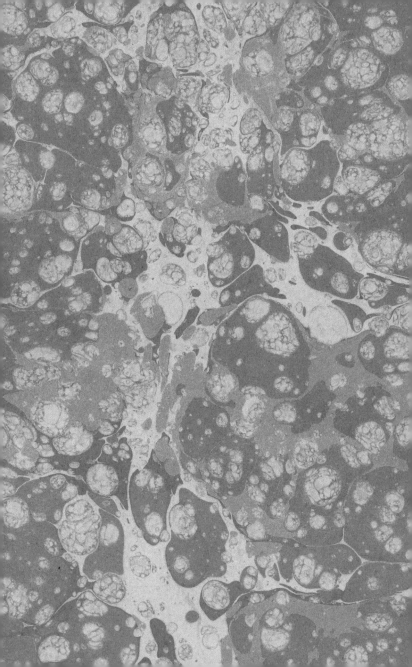

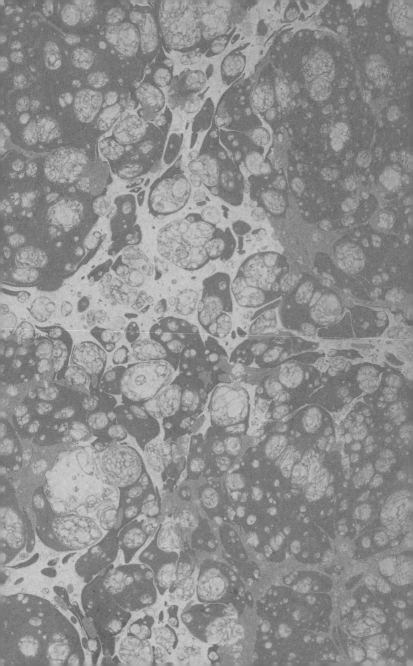

Framed by the church of Santa Trìnita and Palazzo Spini-Feroni, the piazza lies at the top of Florence's most beautiful bridge, which also takes its name from the church, and introduces the city's most famous shopping street, Via Tornabuoni. At times during its long history, this stretch was merely considered a part of Via Tornabuoni, but it certainly fits the medieval definition of a piazza—a widening of the road at a point of intersection. As a result of its relationship with the Santa Trìnita bridge, the church has always been on a main thoroughfare; this is one reason why it became such an important part of the urban landscape.

Even now, more than five hundred years later, the piazza still resembles its portrayal in the Sassetti family chapel found inside Santa Trìnita. Palazzo Spini-Feroni sits to the left side, and the church is on the right, with the bridge between them in the background. While the basic structure was already in place back in the 1480s, new layers have since been added: the church now presents a Baroque façade, the bridge has acquired its graceful curves, and a column rises from the middle of the piazza. Palazzo Spini-Feroni showcases Ferragamo's latest designs in its street-side windows, and a multicoloured sign hanging against the *palazzo* says 'Creativity in Colour', advertising an exhibition of their vast shoe collection, while conjuring up wonderful images and possibilities in my mind. There was a time when only neutrals dominated my life, but now a rainbow of oranges, reds and purples colour everything from my wardrobe and oil paintings to my home.

From my spot on the stone bench I can see the church's sacristy, which is disjointed from the rest of the church; a bank fills the space between them. In the 1420s, Palla Strozzi had appointed Ghiberti, who was busy sculpting his second set of doors for the Battistero at the time, to build the sacristy. One of the church's most beautiful details is the carved marble frame around the door into the sacristy.

While he was having the sacristy built, Palla took the opportunity to memorialise his artistic and cultural ambitions by dedicating the room adjacent to the family chapel to a public library.

A Roman column at the centre of the piazza, topped with a statue of *Justice*, commemorates a victory that Cosimo I's army won at Montemurlo. It seems the more I learn about Florence, the more I see how intrinsically tied the Medici family is to the city's organisation. Piazza Santa Trìnita was among the venues for tournaments and other grand events in the days of the Medici, which is one explanation for this modest piazza assuming such importance. Another reason was that their daily carriage route from Piazza Pitti to the north side of the river passed through Piazza Santa Trìnita—cars follow the same course today—so the Medici enhanced their route with various symbols that celebrated the family's successes. Their carriages would first pass through Piazza San Felice, where Cosimo I had placed the column in memory of his army's victory at Marciano. Piazza San Felice then became a symbolic and visual counterpoint to Piazza Santa Trìnita, with Ponte Santa Trìnita—whose graceful design by Ammannati had been commissioned to celebrate a definitive defeat over Siena—linking the two squares. Even the statues of the four *Seasons* set at each corner were added by the Medici, in honour of Cosimo II's wedding in 1608.

The Vallombrosan church of Santa Trìnita was built on the site of an oratory in the later part of the eleventh century, just outside the Roman boundaries, and was brought within the first set of city walls a century later. Giovanni Gualberto had founded the austere Vallombrosan order in 1040, after beginning his life as a monk with the Benedictines up at San Miniato. He left once he realised they didn't quite meet his expectations for piety; his goal with the Vallombrosan order was to restore the original simplicity that he felt was appropriate, but lacking, in monastic rule at the time.

Santa Trìnita was rebuilt in the mid-thirteenth century, when a city-wide church expansion project was in progress. It assumed a Gothic aspect, with ribbed vaults composed of pointed arches that spring from square piers topped by Corinthian capitals. In the fifteenth century, chapels were inserted into the side walls, with the corner ones opening graciously into both the nave and the transept, and the next several generations of wealthy Florentine families set about commissioning frescoes to decorate them. At one time the entire interior was covered with frescoes, although most have disappeared during the course of various renovations. Many chapels were sponsored by families who were also building their impressive family *palazzi* nearby. The Sassetti chapel is the best known; frescoes by Ghirlandaio incorporated not only the members of distinguished families, but were also set in two of Florence's important piazzas— Piazza Santa Trìnita and Piazza della Signoria.

At the end of the sixteenth century, during a counter- Reformation renovation encouraged by the grand dukes, the Vallombrosans asked Buontalenti to renovate the choir and rebuild the convent in a more sober and imposing style. While Buontalenti's façade proposal had not been selected for the Duomo, he was able to incorporate some of his ideas into the design for Santa Trìnita. His aim was to emphasise the façade's verticality, so he focused on the central section and downplayed the extra width created by the chapels, using subtle double scrolls for the transition between the nave vault and side aisles. Expressing the typical refinement of his work, they are quite unlike the bold volutes found on the façades of Santo Spirito and Santa Maria Novella.

In the 1890s, during an attempt to return the interior to its original medieval form, the church underwent a much debated restoration. Mannerist and Baroque additions were removed, and Buontalenti's sculptural stairs leading up to the altar were transferred to the church of Santo Stefano; more 'suitable' artwork was brought from the nearby San Pancrazio. This swapping of pieces was common among churches. From the church of San Miniato, Santa Trìnita received a miraculous crucifix (whose story unfolds in the Piazzale Michelangelo chapter), but several of its own pieces ended up at other churches or museums—an indication of the importance of the commissions that Santa Trìnita inspired during the Renaissance.

Once again I am sitting on the bench that wraps around the front and south side of Palazzo Bartolini-Salimbeni. Stone benches surround many of the city's old *palazzi*—one way in which this urban feature responded to the needs of the community. Citizens and officials who had business in the palace would sit on the benches as they waited their turn, merchants used them to display their wares and, just like residents and tourists today, anyone could take a break there and watch the world go by.

Many of these *palazzi* also feature architectural details that showcased the skills of the many thriving craftsmen in their day. You can still see iron rings used for tying up horses and also the wrought-iron torch-holders, bestowed by the *Comune* on important families who had performed a public service, which illuminated the streets for everyone.

It was the general climate of prosperity in the fifteenth century that allowed so many noble families to build the *palazzi* that populate Florence. These grand structures represented individuality and power, much in the same way as the towers of the rich families in Florence had done previously. The private palaces also brought an imposing scale to the urban plan, helping to better unify the cluttered blocks of housing that comprised the medieval part of the town, thus becoming reference points within the city. Unfortunately for the poorer citizens, their housing was often obliterated to accommodate these block-sized homes.

It's interesting to search for the links from chapel to artist to patron family to nearby *palazzo*, to see the dissemination of family fortunes and fame throughout the city. A century before asking Baccio d'Agnolo to build their palace in the 1520s, the Bartolini had already commissioned a chapel in Santa Trìnita church. The family's new home opposite the church, with its unusual windows divided by crosses of stone, caused quite a stir among the Florentines. People complained that it looked like a church, but the design was widely copied, and the architect ordered the phrase 'It is easier to criticise than to imitate' to be engraved in Latin over the entrance.

The battlemented Palazzo Spini-Feroni, now home to Ferragamo, dates back to 1289. Along with Palazzo Frescobaldi at the southern end of Ponte Santa Trìnita, it formed part of the bridge's defence system. An arch allowed passage onto Lungarno Acciaioli, the road that runs along this stretch of the river, but the arch and small tower on the Arno were demolished in order to develop the riverfront area in the nineteenth century.

Palazzo Gianfigliazzi sits opposite the Spini palace and was built soon after. To its right is the shop that most fascinates me along this retail heaven: SPACE. It nestles up against the south side of Santa Trìnita, in an improbable sliver of a footprint between the church and the *palazzo*. The space is so narrow that in many parts of the world it would probably be discounted as unusable, except maybe as a repository for rubbish bins or discarded junk. Instead, streamlined shelves of clothing fill the interior, and through the skylight is the surprise of seeing the wall it shares with the church rising overhead.

Several streets radiate outwards from the piazza, offering endless possibilities for meandering: Ponte Santa Trìnita crosses into the Oltrarno, Via Parione leads towards the Carraia bridge, three streets curve eastward to the original part of the city centre. The Strozzi, Davanzati and Rucellai family *palazzi*—each with their own piazza—are also found in this neighbourhood, and of course there's the *palazzo*-lined Via Tornabuoni tempting shoppers as it heads north. Two such palaces, Palazzo Minerbetti and Palazzo Strozzi del Poeta, join on their upper levels to form the lovely Hotel Tornabuoni Beacci.

This is where I stayed my first time in the city centre. The Pensione Bencistà near Fiesole had only a few nights available, so I decided to begin my visit at a hotel in *Centro* for a change. I had heard horror stories about the noise, which seemed an inequitable trade for the Bencistà's tranquil outdoor space, but I knew it would be interesting to have a new perspective, to try a different routine. The commotion of traffic, construction and people was certainly noticeable, but not unreasonable, and the Beacci's rooftop patio turned out to be a great urban alternative to the Bencistà's many terraces. It was wonderful to have a place to retreat right in the city—being able to see workers going about the business of replacing roof tiles, the beauty of all those converging rooflines up close. Birds still came to the breakfast table, the vines offered shade, breezes kept us cool. The rooms were inviting, and full of antiques, and on a later visit we stayed in a room whose ceiling and walls were frescoed to give the impression that we were in an outdoor room in the country. And the hotel's location made it easy to pop out to a museum, for an evening concert in a church, or to try the selection of restaurants.

On my later visits to Florence I usually rented apartments, so the Beacci remains the only hotel in the centre that I can recommend from personal experience. My friends (and their friends) have always been pleased with this choice. When I met a family friend at the Beacci recently, I flipped through one of the old guest books looking for Ella's scribblings from our last visit, remembering the pleasures of staying here. I still dream of returning as a guest one day.

I like to walk along Via Tornabuoni, enjoying the chance to window-shop in the upmarket shopper's paradise, and daydream a little. Would I dare to wear that gold Gucci pantsuit? Any chance the fun Pucci-print dress would suit me? Do they serve breakfast at Tiffany's when you make a purchase?

While they may be housed in some of the city's oldest *palazzi*, the famous designer-name shops are all about the current art of fashion and design. Whether along Via Tornabuoni or on a narrow side street selling a mix of treasures—engravings, textiles, books, decorative hardware, hand-printed paper, original art—the window displays tend towards works of art themselves. At once attractive, provocative, original and trendy, for me they are the main appeal of the luxurious shops in Piazza Santa Trìnita and along Via Tornabuoni. I draw inspiration from the colours, the fabrics, the twists on the classics, and my mind turns over the possibilities for transforming the fashions—sometimes outlandish, other times incredibly clever—into another creative idea. The pattern of a Ferragamo blouse inspires a collage, the mannequin wearing the Pucci kaftan comes to life as a social butterfly who gaily passes around drinks during cocktail hour in her sprawling country villa.

I'm drawn to the vignettes set up in the windows. One shop has devoted a display to author Jack Kerouac. There's a simple but beautifully detailed bomber jacket, casual but stylish-looking suede boots, a great leather bag (the kind you throw everything into at a moment's notice, and then take off for somewhere exotic)—signature pieces that represent the writer's life, or at least the one being promoted. At another shop a beautifully detailed arched window frames a mannequin who looks as if she's going on a different sort of trip: wearing impossibly high-heeled patent leather boots, she's dressed in an elegant black coat with a knit shawl collar. A stack of chocolate-brown leather luggage—the sort you wouldn't think of checking on a plane anymore—sits next to her, and thrown on top is the creamy mohair sweater that she will don once she's boarded the Orient Express.

One reason for the eye-catching windows may be that the Florentines have a different shopping mentality: they are happy to window-shop, but if they enter a store it usually means they know exactly what they intend to buy. Many shops have begun posting signs that say 'free entry'; you will see them even at a tiny produce store, and wonder, 'Why on earth *wouldn't* it be free to go in and look at the fruit?' I think they intend it as more of an invitation to check out their goods, which apparently is counter-cultural.

Our neighbours from the United States spent a day in Florence last time they were in Tuscany, and I finally had my first proper experience in a Via Tornabuoni shop. Jenny wanted to visit Loretta Caponi, where Ella and I had admired the precious christening gowns and eyelet dresses many times from the street. The shop is filled with an air of old-world luxury, from the beautifully worn wooden floors to the old-fashioned toy that creaked loudly as Jenny's older daughter rocked noisily back and forth. It's a lovely space for the fine fabrics that have been turned into women's dressing gowns, textiles for the home and children's clothing. Besides seeing and feeling the patterned heirloom fabrics that had been turned into gorgeous children's tops, the best part of the experience was watching the saleswoman blossom in the presence of a customer who wanted to do more than 'just look'.

I think about where I would choose to set up my own personal vignette—probably in one of the stationery shops found on the streets leading off Piazza Santa Trinita. There would be a journal covered with marbled paper, with a tooled leather spine, my fountain pen with the lustre of brown- and black-speckled tortoiseshell, the brown leather book bag I bought at the Mercato Nuovo on my first visit to Florence, a shelf of favourite books ... Perhaps this concept of the vignette is a contemporary version of the Renaissance portrait, in which the subjects were often painted with significant items from their lives. Long before that, when art was mostly religious, saints were often identified by a relevant symbol, and even in ancient times, people were inclined to enter the afterlife accompanied by meaningful objects from their earthly lives.

I enjoy the display windows of homeware shops too. At the top of Via Tornabuoni is an inviting shop where the tables are always set with pretty crockery, table linens and cutlery. A beautiful table can be a work of art and, in fact, I am fascinated by the idea of painting a dinner party, with the table as the framework for portraying the diners. Viewed from above and with only the place settings and hands of the guests visible, it would be more of a character study. Hands reveal so much about us—the jewellery we wear, our choice of watch (or maybe the absence of one), the state of the hands themselves. And then there's the question of the food: do we finish every bite and place the silverware neatly once we've finished, leave a bite or two to be polite, ignore the peas and devour the potatoes? It would be interesting to portray the course of a meal with a series of 'snapshots' as the evening progressed. I find this concept of snapshots, of capturing moments with sketches, paintings or photographs, quite intriguing. They may seem to tell the story, but snapshots never reveal the whole story—merely isolated moments of a multidimensional life, or city or trip.

On a rainy winter evening I take refuge in Santa Trìnita church. The dim pendant lamps in a chapel near the altar glow in the gloom, creating the setting for a gold-framed crucifix, and trays of candles glow eerily before altars. The voices of two women in the front pew startle me when they begin wailing the rosary.

This is a true urban church, in that you can quickly pop in for a few minutes in the morning or after the *pausa*, or during the evening's chanting of the rosary or vespers. I like standing at the interior glass door, watching the pedestrians going past outside, on their way home from work, to meet friends for an *aperitivo*, or with their arms adorned by designer bags from a shopping expedition. Across the street is Ferragamo, in all its elegance, with a stone plaque that reads 'Salvatore Ferragamo, S.p.A.', looking as if it has been there since the *palazzo* was first built.

To finish the rosary the women repeat '*Pregha per noi*', 'Pray for us', over and over. What are their sins? The priest who attends them disappears, and a hooded monk soon emerges from a door opening onto the main altar, then removes his hood. For vespers he is joined only by the priest from the rosary, but speakers amplify their voices through the church. The faithful sit at the front, while several people wander through the basilica. I can't take my eyes off a lady in shimmery jeans. She is wearing the pointiest turquoise high-heeled pumps I have ever seen, resting them delicately on the kneeling bench before her.

Even during mass, people mill about: guides deliver historical details about the church, the serious visitors are intent on their guidebooks, others flock to Ghirlandaio's frescoes. The priest from the *rosario* seems very fidgety; he keeps looking at the ceiling, can't seem to keep his arms still. It's not the same meditative experience as attending vespers up at San Miniato, the church where San Gualberto began his career as a monk.

In my continuing search for paintings with the Annunciation theme, I find three before the altars along the left aisle. In the fourth chapel from the door, the Bartolini-Salimbeni chapel, Lorenzo Monaco's *Annunciation* from the 1420s is very graceful and controlled; although poor Mary would bump her head on the ceiling if she stood up. (This was a common flaw of paintings when the laws of perspective were still relatively new.) A century later, Michele Tosini also incorporated architecture to frame the scene.

His angel really 'says' to a gracious Mary, 'Wait. Just listen to me for a moment.' In the first chapel on the left, the Antica Cappella degli Strozzi, is the latest of the three—Jacopo da Empoli painted this very different *Annunciation* in 1603. Mary and Gabriel are no longer contained within an architectural setting, and the enormity of the canvas makes the dramatic light and shadow of the *chiaroscuro* effect even more pronounced.

This church is small enough that you can really get to know it well; you can easily return to the various chapels to reconsider them in the light of one another. Yet there's still a lot to see. Despite the many updates and restorations, traces of the Romanesque counter-façade are still visible on the entrance wall. The interior recalls the church of Santa Maria Novella—only on a more intimate scale—and here the painted stripes that define the ribs of the vaulting are slowly being whitewashed. The space is rational, with a sense of order; there's none of the drama of the Baroque interior of San Gaetano at the other end of Via Tornabuoni. Perhaps moving Buontalenti's steps to the larger church of Santo Stefano was a wise choice; they may very well have been too overwhelming for this space.

Piazza Santa Trìnita is so much more than a road, more than just another place to walk through on my way to somewhere else. Each time I cross Ponte Santa Trìnita, I look forward to the first glimpse of Santa Trìnita's façade, as the sun glances on the stone exterior, revealing its warm stone detailing. On my way back from the plant market in Piazza della Repubblica, I like to pick up a *caprese* sandwich at Bar Parione just off the square, and sit among the people on

Palazzo Bartolini-Salimbeni's bench. And whether I'm following this former Medici route into the city or towards home, I take pleasure in walking past the grand old palaces, in remembering my stays at the Beacci—and noticing the latest fantastic patterned creation to show up in Pucci's window.

# Piazza di San Lorenzo

All year long, Piazza San Lorenzo teems with tourists visiting the church complex and browsing the outdoor market, and August is no exception. The city's residents, however, are winding down for their holiday on the fifteenth, when just about the whole country shuts down. The Italians have been taking Ferragosto, the 'August holidays', since Roman times, and Catholics also observe the Feast of the Assumption, which marks Mary's ascension into heaven, on the fifteenth of August. In any case, every Italian who is able will flee to the mountains or seaside to escape the heat and the foreign visitors who take over their cities, leaving Florence in the awkward position of hosting the summer crowds with fewer shops, restaurants and proprietors to accommodate them.

I had always been warned that August was the worst time to come to Florence, but my curiosity finally got the better of me one year. It turned out to be a record-breaking August, but I enjoyed seeing a new side of the city. And now that I live here I appreciate the month's different rhythm—although I still feel compelled to list the drawbacks when friends or family are contemplating a visit.

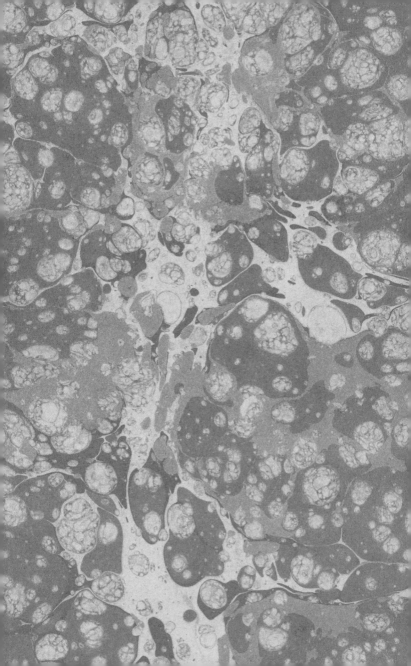

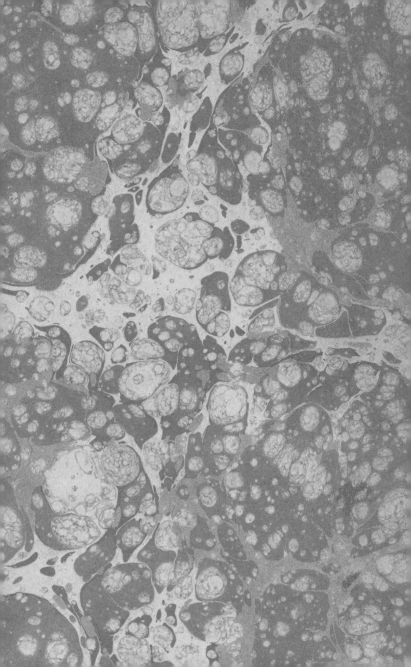

Today is 10 August, the feast day of the patron saint of San Lorenzo church, a celebration I look forward to each year. From Piazza San Giovanni I follow the parade of Florentines in historic costume to San Lorenzo, wondering how they can bear to wear their velvets, brocades and feather headdresses on such a muggy and oppressive day. In the morning special masses are held in honour of San Lorenzo, and that evening I return to the church to hear the ebullient prior thanking the residents who stick around for this holiday that 'cuts the monotony of the summer'. He introduces the Filarmonica di Firenze 'Gioacchino Rossini', commonly known as the Banda Rossini—a one-hundred-and-fifty-year-old philharmonic orchestra that plays on many of Florence's important holidays. As the musicians make their way through the evening's program from their stage on the raised area in front of the church, along the side volunteers prepare bowls of pasta and slices of watermelon for everyone. They serve the eager crowds tirelessly, while the piazza grows sticky with watermelon juice and seeds, making me wonder if the construction workers who took up the paving stones recently found the seeds that must disappear into the crevices.

The church's namesake was a third-century Christian martyr. According to legend, as punishment for being impudent to the Emperor Valerian, Lorenzo was roasted instead of beheaded, the more common method of execution at the time—and that after being 'cooked' on one side, Lorenzo pointed out, with a touch of ironic humour, that it was time he was turned over. (I suppose we must remember that these soon-to-be saints were in a hurry to get to heaven.) As the archivist and librarian for the church during his lifetime, San Lorenzo became the patron saint of libraries and librarians, but cooks also claim him as theirs because of his legendary means of martyrdom. The falling stars from the annual Perseids meteor shower, which fills the night skies each year around the time of San Lorenzo's feast day, are poetically known as the tears of San Lorenzo. After experiencing the celebration in his honour, the tear-shaped watermelon seeds make me think of him too.

Even today, reminders of the Medici family dominate the area around Piazza San Lorenzo, although the original church facing this piazza dates back to a millennium before the Medici quietly began to assume control over Florence. Giovanni di Bicci de' Medici, to whom we trace the two branches of the family, was already buying property in this area in the fourteenth century. When the Medici emerged as a powerful influence in the following century and started developing ties with this neighbourhood, the church of San Lorenzo began to benefit from their commissions. While the family lived in various quarters of the city over their long period of rule, San Lorenzo remained a constant gathering place for the family's energy, funds and bones. Their patronage was bestowed upon the greatest architects and artists over the course of many generations, and the funerary monuments they requested grew more elaborate with each century.

The original church was consecrated by Bishop Ambrose in 393, and served as Florence's cathedral for several centuries. It was rebuilt in the second half of the eleventh century, and then, like the other major churches, brought within the communal walls of 1173. The Medici set a major renewal scheme into motion in the 1420s, when Giovanni di Bicci commissioned Brunelleschi to build the sacristy (which became known as the Old Sacristy once Michelangelo built the 'New' one a century later), and chapels endowed by other prominent families and decorated by a variety of artists soon followed. Giovanni's eldest son, Cosimo il Vecchio, asked Brunelleschi to update the church's interior later that decade; it was the first to be redesigned in the Renaissance style.

I have always been fascinated by how the serene basilica presents such an unexpected contrast with the church's façade: the carefully designed interior is concealed by a façade that remains unfinished to this day, and offers but few clues to the interior. I rather like this incongruity that exists between many of the church interiors and their exteriors; it adds an element of mystery that only reveals itself once you go inside.

In the sixteenth century, Michelangelo, along with several other architects, proposed an elaborate façade project for San Lorenzo. His internal façade was built, but the execution of the exterior was abandoned in favour of other commissions, leaving the rows of stone and brick exposed. In February 2007 Michelangelo's façade design was projected onto the church for a month's worth of weekend nights, reminiscent of Mario Mariotti's façade event in Piazza Santo Spirito. The inauguration was held on the anniversary of the death of the last living Medici, Anna Maria Luisa, which also marked two hundred and seventy years since the *Patto di Famiglia* was signed; in this document Anna Maria Luisa bequeathed the entire Medici legacy to the city of Florence.

Although highly refined (in keeping with the church's interior), Michelangelo's horizontal rectangular form had altogether ignored the present shape, which at least reflects the interior's high nave flanked by lower aisles. During the celebration honouring Anna Maria Luisa, a seven-metre-long marble column was displayed alongside the basilica; one of three found near the town of Pietrasanta in 1998, it had apparently been intended by Michelangelo for his façade. It was interesting to see the juxtaposition of the white marble next to the rough stone that it would have obscured.

As with the church of Santo Spirito, I feel that San Lorenzo's façade should keep its unadorned aspect. The façade's orderly but slightly varied rows of stone create an appealing pattern of relief and recess, alternately capturing the light and casting shadows. Local author Professor Giovanni Fanelli summed up the Florentines beautifully when he compared them to Florence's unfinished church façades; their understated simplicity and unadorned beauty seem to perfectly describe the Florentine spirit.

The piazza and its snaking lines of market stands flow around the three open sides of the church complex. Piazza San Lorenzo is quite different from the squares that lie before the Medici family's later homes in Piazza della Signoria and Piazza Pitti. It's comparatively small; until the last century buildings enveloped most of the church and only the rough façade emerged from the urban fabric. In the corner of the piazza nearest the Medici family home is a statue of Giovanni delle Bande Nere, by reputation a brave and brutal warrior who died in combat before his thirtieth birthday. A descendant of the cadet branch of the Medici (the line descended from Cosimo il Vecchio's younger brother, Lorenzo), he was the father of Cosimo I, who was recruited to power in 1537 and went on to become the first grand duke of Tuscany.

While I pass through the piazza regularly, and pause in the adjoining cloister whenever I have time, I no longer tend to pay a casual visit to the church; like a number of other church complexes, San Lorenzo has started charging a small admission fee. The church really merits more than a quick look around though: as with Brunelleschi's other buildings, this space invites contemplation.

There are many chapels to linger before, as well as Brunelleschi's sacristy, Donatello's bronze pulpits, a wall-sized painting by Agnolo Bronzino, showing the martyrdom of San Lorenzo in Mannerist proportions, and Desiderio da Settignano's angelic expressions sculpted in marble for the Altar of the Sacrament.

Brunelleschi integrated his classically influenced design principles into a spacious and well balanced volume, creating a fitting space for the treasure trove San Lorenzo would become as the century progressed. The basilica is very similar to that of Santo Spirito, which the architect would begin a decade later. I'm intrigued by the differences, though: how the orientation in relation to the sun changes the atmosphere within each interior—Santo Spirito faces towards the south, San Lorenzo to the east; how Santo Spirito has the enormous *baldacchino*, which can feel like such an interruption—yet when I walk into San Lorenzo I can't help but note its absence. The detailing is richer at San Lorenzo, no doubt a result of the Medici influence.

I always look forward to seeing the painting by Pietro Annigoni in one of the side chapels. The artist shows Jesus as a boy in his father's carpentry workshop, one of those rare moments where Joseph is seen in his role as an ordinary father. The colours and the light, especially as it falls on Jesus, are stunning. Painted in 1964, this is a much newer piece in comparison to the centuries-old paintings in the other chapels and, as always, I enjoy finding the work of more recent artists forming a new layer in this Renaissance city.

The Medici of the fourteenth century are commemorated in the Old Sacristy, found off the church's south transept. While Brunelleschi created the beautifully proportioned architectural space, his friend Donatello attended to many of the decorative details, including the tomb that Cosimo il Vecchio (not to be confused with the first grand duke, Cosimo I) commissioned for his parents, Giovanni di Bicci and Piccarda de' Medici. The sacristy also contains a monument to

Cosimo il Vecchio's sons, Giovanni and Piero il Gottoso (Piero the Gouty). Lorenzo and his brother Giovanni—the one murdered in the Pazzi conspiracy—were originally buried here, but their bodies were later moved to the New Sacristy.

To visit the New Sacristy, you must leave the church and find the entrance to the Cappelle Medicee, a state-run museum in charge of both the New Sacristy and the Cappella dei Principi. It's worth the diversion to see how the later Medici tombs differ from the early ones. First, in the 1520s, Michelangelo began the New Sacristy, designing the space as a counterpoint to the Old Sacristy. He also created the entire sculptural program for this project, which includes a complex family tree of Giulios, Giulianos, Giovannis and Lorenzos. I am still trying to grasp the unwieldy Medici family tree. My daughter summed it up when she saw a diagram showing the many generations of the two branches of Medici: 'That's *really* big'.

It was Pope Clement VII—Lorenzo il Magnifico's nephew, christened Giulio de' Medici—who ordered Michelangelo to construct the New Sacristy. This took him away from his work on the church façade, which had previously been commissioned by Pope Leo X—Clement VII's predecessor and cousin, Giovanni de' Medici, who was Lorenzo il Magnifico's second son—and is one reason the façade was never finished.

Within Michelangelo's famous tombs, featuring *Day* and *Night* and *Dawn* and *Dusk*, are Lorenzo il Magnifico's third-born son Giuliano and grandson Lorenzo (son of first-born Piero). Respected and much adored for his humane disposition, Giuliano died of tuberculosis in 1516 at the age of only thirty-seven. Giuliano, who became Duke of Nemours, is shown as 'Action', with figures representing 'Night' and 'Day' below. While *Night* is highly polished, *Day* remains rough; Michelangelo never had a chance to finish it.

On the opposite wall, 'Thought'—with figures portraying Dawn and Dusk below him—personifies Lorenzo, Duke of Urbino. He was the father of Catherine de' Medici (who grew up to become Queen of France), although both he and the baby's mother died in 1519, within a few weeks of her birth. It was to Lorenzo, the last male of the senior line of Medici, that Machiavelli dedicated *The Prince*. Dawn, shown just awakening, the day ahead still full of possibilities, is the most graceful and polished of the quartet of allegorical statues.

Sketches by Michelangelo cover the walls of the altar niche, which lies between the elaborate tombs for the Duke of Nemours and the Duke of Urbino. Opposite the altar, within an unassuming tomb decorated by statues of Saint Damien and Saint Cosmos flanking Mary, are the remains of Lorenzo and his brother Giuliano; they were brought here from the Old Sacristy in 1559.

The later Medici generations, who became grand dukes, are commemorated under the enormous terracotta-tiled dome. Although its size leads some people to mistake it for Brunelleschi's cupola, a notable difference is the absence of the lantern. While never executed, the intended lantern can be seen crowning the impressive model of the Cappella dei Principi; it's on display in the crypt, where members of the cadet branch of the Medici are buried. The opulent chapel is decorated entirely with inlaid *pietre dure*, with the many colours of stone creating a riot of marble patterns in a cacophony of colours.

This 'Chapel of the Princes' was begun in the early seventeenth century, and here the family's ease in demonstrating their power and wealth is evident, especially when you consider that the chapel is only a partial realisation of the family's aspirations. It's interesting to note that, although San Lorenzo church's floor area is considerably larger than the Chapel of the Princes, the overall scale is markedly more sensitive and subtle in comparison.

If you consider the funerary monument of Cosimo il Vecchio (the head of the senior branch of the family) in the light of the Chapel of the Princes, the change—and the contrast—becomes clear. Once he had ensured that his parents and sons would be commemorated in the elegant and restrained Old Sacristy, he chose for himself only a discreet tomb below the pavement of San Lorenzo's nave, near the altar: quietly positioned at the centre after death, much as he had lived his life.

After leaving the Cappelle Medicee, I like to stop off at La Casa del Vino for a sandwich and a *bicchiere di vino rosso*, as a way of recalibrating myself after experiencing the almost mind-numbing grandeur and ostentation of the later Medici burial temples. Tucked away behind the chaotic market-stand route, and always crowded with office workers at lunchtime, the cosy shop features a classic marble bar and floor-to-ceiling shelves of dark wood. You can order a fresh crusty roll filled with almost anything you might wish for, then complement it with a flute of sparkling prosecco, a glass of house red or any of a number of special vintages.

A similar contrast to that between San Lorenzo's exterior and its interior is also found between the piazza and the church's cloister. While even the largest of the piazzas can feel over-crowded in the busiest season, the cloisters possess a more serene character, retaining their associations with tranquillity and meditation. Michelangelo's tombs for the New Sacristy could be used to illustrate the relationship between the character of a piazza and a cloister: the piazza is personified by 'Action', while the cloister embodies 'Thought'.

San Lorenzo's cloister is very much an urban one. The entrance is through a portal at the left of the church and, with no fees to pay and no circuitous entries or lines to negotiate, you can easily wander in from the bustle of the piazza. Simple cross vaults in the loggia create a harmonious rhythm around the entire cloister, and at the centre is an ancient multi-trunked orange tree, home to the twittering birds who help drown out the commotion in the piazza.

My mind can't help but wander to other possibilities for using such a perfect architectural space: it would make a lovely trattoria or herb garden, provide a peaceful setting for a swimming pool or a playground; parents could sit under the loggia, companionably drinking tea. I think of the four stages of a day as portrayed by Michelangelo's sculptures—dawn, day, dusk and night—and how a home built around a cloister could be organised according to the phases we move through every twenty-four hours. Each side could variously accommodate morning, afternoon, evening and night. Or maybe the architectural elements of a cloister could be constructed using nature's materials—trees and shrubs, wisteria vines and rambling roses.

On the second level of the cloister is another treasure in this complex: the Biblioteca Laurenziana. In the vestibule, a Mannerist staircase by Michelangelo ushers visitors up into the library, which was built to house volumes collected by Cosimo il Vecchio and his grandson Lorenzo il Magnifico. The staircase shows how Michelangelo's sculptural abilities extended not just into painting, but also into architecture; no doubt it inspired Buontalenti when he created his altar steps for the church of Santa Trìnita.

Cosimo il Vecchio began sprucing up the San Lorenzo neighbourhood when he built his family home a stone's throw away from the church, after accepting Michelozzo's design over the one by Brunelleschi (which he had claimed was too grand). Although never a modest building to begin with, the *palazzo* we see today has been considerably enlarged since Cosimo commissioned it. The present name, Palazzo Medici-Riccardi, dates back to the period when the Riccardi family purchased it from the Medici in the mid-sixteenth century.

The palace sits diagonally opposite the church, with a back entrance through the lovely garden just off the piazza; the main entrance on the other side of the block. Michelozzo's design, which was frequently borrowed by the designers of future *palazzi*, divided the façade into three distinctive levels: a heavily rusticated ground floor gives way to a lighter treatment on each subsequent storey, and is finally topped by an elaborate cornice with a generous overhang that keeps passers-by dry in the rain.

The highlight of a visit to the *palazzo* today is the Cappella dei Magi, where Benozzo Gozzoli's colourful and joyful fresco of the procession of the Magi is tucked away in the family's private chapel; several of the Medici are depicted among the dozens of faces. Another spot where I like to sneak a peek is a tiny upper balcony that overlooks the back courtyard, dotted with statues and potted lemon trees; from here I can imagine Lorenzo il Magnifico looking over at the church where his family worshipped and his ancestors were buried.

A market of clothes, tourist knick-knacks and leather bags, jackets and accessories surrounds the church and spills into the neighbouring streets. As one of the biggest concentrations of leather goods in the city, this area is always full of tourists—and illegal hawkers trying to entice people to buy their fake watches, at the risk of all parties being caught and fined.

Following the long jumble of stalls a few blocks north-west takes me to Mercato Centrale, the central food market, which is filled with culinary delights and sensory shocks in the form of dead chickens, rabbits and the innards of any animal considered edible. This two-storey nineteenth-century building of cast iron and glass replaced the open-air Mercato Vecchio after it was torn down. I come here for pecans when I want to make my grandmother's tea biscuits, or to pick up hard-to-find ingredients for ethnic dishes in one fell swoop. It's also a good place to buy small gifts: limoncello, panforte, sun-dried tomatoes, Italian condiments.

Via de' Ginori offers another kind of shopping experience. Leading north out of Piazza San Lorenzo, it offers a variety of one-of-a-kind shops selling beautiful textiles and accessories, stationery and hand-bound books, ethnic clothing and homewares, musical instruments and toys. This narrow street also provides a quieter route to Piazza San Marco, yet another piazza forever connected to the Medici family.

Over the course of three centuries, the Medici dynasty provided sixty-one *Priori*, thirty-five *Gonfalonieri*, seven grand dukes and two popes. But when Lorenzo il Magnifico died in 1492, leaving only his son, the politically inept Piero il Fatuo—Piero the Unfortunate—to take charge, for several years Florence fell under the influence of the intense Fra Savonarola, whose story unfolds in Piazza San Marco.

# Piazza di San Marco

Piazza San Marco lies north of the religious centre, at the end of Via Cavour, once known as Via Larga. This so-called 'wide' road linked the Medici palace with yet another church that benefited from their patronage—San Marco. Its understated Baroque façade harmonises with the simplicity of this convent that knew both the gentle hand of Fra Angelico and the fanatical grip of the austere Girolamo Savonarola; only a few statues, bas reliefs and decorative details.

The Dominican church complex quietly graces one side of this shady square, which hums with university students and crowds of bus commuters. A statue of Italian general Manfredo Fanti stands at the centre, benches sit before the hedges and trees that enclose each corner and a tight ring of Vespas parked perpendicularly to the kerb separates the traffic that flies around the pedestrian centre. A rectangle of buildings defines the edges, broken by six busy roads running in and out of the piazza.

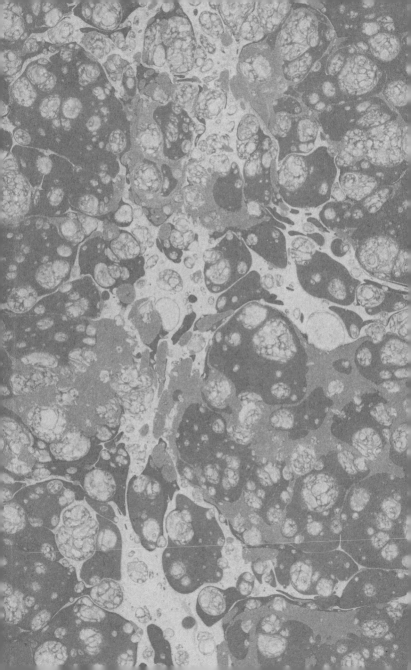

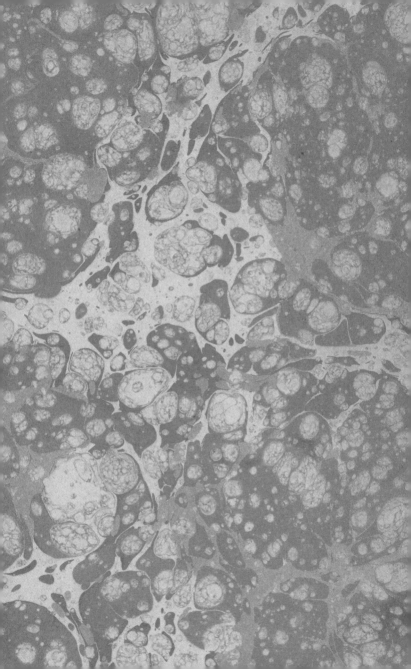

This is about as far north as my regular routine usually takes me. At one time the area was considered a village on its own—Cafaggio—so the square was known as Piazza San Marco in Cafaggio. While it's only another five minutes' walk beyond San Lorenzo, many visitors don't make it this far north; the original limits of the first communal walls seem to serve as a kind of invisible boundary.

The church has its roots in a twelfth-century oratory dedicated to San Marco. The Silvestrines built a convent here in 1299, but for a host of political reasons—think Medici—the Dominicans of Fiesole were given the church and dilapidated complex in 1435. Cosimo il Vecchio pledged his generous support, and asked Michelozzo, his favourite architect, to rebuild the church and monastery.

While I do not enjoy this church interior as much as Florence's others—the atmosphere is not as welcoming and the Baroque decor that was added in the eighteenth century is not to my taste—the convent next door is always a pleasure to visit. The assorted ground-floor rooms and cells upstairs are open to the public through the state-run Museo di San Marco.

The cloister is built around a single Lebanese cedar, whose trunk reaches high before spreading its boughs to shelter the garden. A climbing rose rambles up the trunk, and colourful annuals, out of scale with the tree, border the edges. You can still see traces of the Gothic windows along the side of the church, a reminder that it was not always characterised by the ornate Baroque interior. The brick detailing under the roofline of the monks' cells on the upper level is gorgeous; while the undersides of the roof overhangs are often an interesting part of Florence's Renaissance buildings, finding one in brick is unusual.

The group of Reformed Dominicans who came down to San Marco from the nearby hilltop town of Fiesole in 1435 had been hoping to secure a site in the city so they could more easily spread their message of renewal. Among them was Fra Giovanni, or Fra Angelico as he came to be known, who for eight years led a team of his brothers in creating the simple but powerful frescoes in the cells, the cloister and the chapter house. A young Benozzo Gozzoli also helped; this was before he created the much-lauded procession of the Magi in the chapel at Palazzo Medici, where the influence of his time spent with Fra Angelico is evident. The beloved friar is considered the patron saint of artists, and his presence is palpable throughout the convent, making me feel more favourably disposed towards the strict Dominicans.

Sitting in the cloister or walking through the lofty halls of San Marco's cells seems to inspire contemplation. This morning, students on a field trip are seated around the ledge that surrounds the cloister's garden, writing and sketching in their journals. Like me, they appear intent on introspection, jotting down whatever thoughts may come.

Fra Angelico's *Annunciation* is at the top of the stairs that lead up to the cells; this serene fresco would have greeted the brothers each time they retired here for prayer, meditation or sleep. The frescoes in the cells are characterised by more restrained colour and style than the paintings intended for public areas, and are distinctive for a couple of reasons. Unlike many works that have been swapped from one church to another, or placed in museum collections, they have survived in their intended context. Their function, too, was different to the religious frescoes typically found in churches. Instead of being designed to educate a faithful congregation, their sole purpose was to inspire prayer and meditation in the friars.

The convent seems like a natural place to consider the idea of retreat. Nowadays many religious communities allow visitors to take advantage of their peaceful settings when they need a reprieve from everyday life; Cosimo il Vecchio had a double cell at San Marco for this purpose. At the risk of sounding ascetic, I wouldn't turn down a cell at San Marco. Each one has a lovely terracotta floor, a barrel-vaulted ceiling and a niched window, and the corridor, with its wooden-raftered ceiling, is a pleasure to walk along. My choice would be a south-facing cell overlooking the cloister; there's a double one with a fresco of Jesus surrounded by his disciples—a positive image that calls to mind a circle for discussion, and which would be infinitely preferable to the bloody crucifixions portrayed in many of the cells.

When I dream about a retreat, it's not necessarily a monk's cell that comes to mind though—neither is it massages, pedicures and facials—but another kind of pampering and rejuvenation that I crave. My mind wanders to thoughts of the Pensione Bencistà ... being surrounded by the cypresses and olives of the countryside; having breakfast, lunch and tea on the terrace; dinner in the grand hall—and with no chores or other distractions competing with time for being creative. Instead of appointments for saunas, yoga and meditation, I would schedule time with my journal, my art kit, my favourite books. I never cease to be educated, absorbed, baffled, energised and inspired by others, but give me a pen and my journal, the hours stretching far ahead, and I am content.

Creating and being a great mother are my main focuses for the moment—a synergistic goal. I love how Ella shares the studio with me, using my colours, papers and book-binding tools for projects of her own. Finding time for all the creative activities I want to do with her is not always easy though—they often take a back seat to the logistics of running our lives, to social obligations and to-do lists.

I struggle constantly with my need for solitude, which reminds me of Anne Morrow Lindbergh's *Gift from the Sea*. She believed that, while women may always be on call—whether at home or work, as mothers, daughters, partners or friends—it's important to spend some time alone each day, every week, and once a year. She found it's often not just the being on-call aspect that prevents women from finding this time to be alone. Lindbergh points out that an appointment for solitude isn't regarded with the same respect as one for a haircut, lunch with a friend or a work-related engagement—in short, any occasion in which you have committed to another person. But, as she says, to merely have an appointment with yourself is akin to admitting to a 'secret vice'.

I try to keep her advice in mind: once a day, once a week, once a year. Each day and each week are possible, and now that my husband and I are no longer together, the annual interlude of solitude has also become a reality. While the days of my daughter's absence always feel strange, these brief periods invariably prove to be a time of renewal—a chance to reconsider my dreams, to make a leap creatively.

Standing in Savonarola's cell, I couldn't be further from the concept of indulging in my creativity. With the sound of traffic rushing through the open window, I try to imagine what went through the priest's head as he prayed, worked and slept in these rooms.

Savonarola first came to San Marco in 1481. His eloquent sermons against luxury, vice and worldliness became increasingly popular, and within the decade he was appointed the prior of San

Marco. After Lorenzo il Magnifico's death in 1492, followed by the exile of the Medici family in 1494, Savonarola became the spiritual ruler of the city. At his command, citizens sacrificed their wigs, books and jewels in the Bonfire of the Vanities. Botticelli, who grew increasingly more religious in his later years, even added some of his paintings to the bonfire. When Savonarola accurately predicted that Charles VIII of France would invade Italy, it further established his credibility in the eyes of the citizens. Savonarola then gave his support to Charles, in the hope that the king would help establish a democratic government in Florence and also reform the court of Pope Alexander VI, which he deemed corrupt.

Naturally, the Pope was insulted at Savonarola's insinuation of corruption, so he forbade Savonarola to preach. Savonarola continued regardless, and was finally excommunicated for disobedience in 1497. Unfortunately for Savonarola, by then the people of Florence had tired of the severe prior's demands and began to turn against him. In March 1498, the *Comune*, which was being threatened by a papal interdict because of Savonarola's refusal to obey, requested he stop preaching, but to no avail. Savonarola and two of his disciples were finally arrested and, under torture, Savonarola allegedly confessed to being a false prophet. The three were then burned at the stake in Piazza della Signoria, the same square where the Bonfire of the Vanities had blazed the year before.

On 23 May, the anniversary of Savonarola's death, he is honoured by an event known as the *Fiorita*: a special mass is said in his name, there is a parade with the usual Florentines in historic costume, and an enormous wreath of roses is placed on the granite circle that marks his execution site. The procession heads to Ponte Vecchio, where rose petals are strewn on the river, and then the entourage returns to Piazza della Signoria for the commemorative speech.

An unrelated museum, the Museo di Firenze Antica, occupies the ground level of the library wing, which used to be the visitors' dormitory. A very detailed large-scale plan portrays the city centre before the late-nineteenth-century urban redevelopment, naming the countless towers, houses and churches that were destroyed in the demolition. The walls are covered with fragments from some of the buildings destroyed during the restructuring of the Mercato Vecchio area. A set of Gothic windows salvaged from the old archbishop's complex stands out from the many beautifully detailed cornices, columns and capitals. The brickwork is the window's most beautiful feature: some of the individual bricks have designs along their faces, each different. In contrast, the present day Palazzo dell'Arcivescovado in Piazza San Giovanni is faced with plaster—nothing like the building from which this window surround came.

After leaving the museum on the northern side of the block and walking back around to the piazza, I like to pick up a piece of *schiacciata* (the wonderful 'squished' bread) or a slice of pizza from Pugi. I join the other picnickers in the piazza and take some time to look around at the various buildings that make up Piazza San Marco.

This area has retained its cultural and intellectual ties since the days when the Medici occupied this part of the city. Beginning with the renovation of the convent, which is intrinsically linked with the growing interest of the humanities in Florence, the Medici inspired a long tradition of learning and culture: Cosimo il Vecchio was meeting here with the Platonic Society while Fra Angelico was decorating the monastery with his frescoes and oil paintings. Once the cells were completed, Cosimo commissioned Michelozzo to create a public library to house a collection of codices. Later, Pico Mirandola and Agnolo Poliziano were involved with Lorenzo il Magnifico in the Neo-Platonic Academy of Florence, which sometimes met at the complex; the two humanists were both subsequently buried at San Marco.

Across the street from the west side of the church was once the garden of the Academy of San Marco where, thanks to Lorenzo's encouragement, Michelangelo began his studies in sculpture. The neighbourhood continued to be favoured by artists, and the tradition lives on with the vast Accademia dell'Arti di Disegno, which fills the square's south-eastern block. The complex also includes the famous Accademia museum, where Michelangelo's original *David* can be seen, and a *liceo artistico*, a high school emphasising the arts. Filling the south-western block is the ex-Convent of Santa Caterina, which was also taken over by the Accademia di Belle Arti for a period before the Comando Militare turned it into a barracks.

On the north-eastern corner is a branch of the Università degli Studi, which hosts several sections of the Museo di Storia Naturale: Botany, Geology and Palaeontology, Mineralogy and Lithology. The Botanical Garden, instituted by Cosimo I in 1545, lies beyond the university; it formed the original nucleus for the Museum of Natural History when Grand Duke Pietro Leopoldo founded it in 1775. That same year, the grand duke formed another connection with Piazza San Marco when he had a neoclassic *palazzina* built on the west side of the square. Originally destined as grand ducal offices, he decided instead to offer it to his mistress, dancer Livia Raimondi, so it became known as the Casino di Livia.

Another grand ducal love affair had unfolded in this piazza two centuries earlier. Francesco I de' Medici, who kept his alchemy laboratories in the former garden of the Academy of San Marco, spotted Bianca Cappello at her home at number 21 and fell in love with her. The pair caused quite a scandal, especially when Bianca graduated from being his mistress to his wife upon the early death of Francesco's first wife, Giovanna d'Austria. Francesco and Bianca enjoyed nearly a decade together before they both died within a day of one another. At the time, malaria was given as the cause of the their deaths, but of course everyone suspected poison and, indeed, scientific analysis definitively confirmed the presence of arsenic in 2006.

Whenever I come to Piazza San Marco I can't help but remember all the times I caught the bus here to head 'home' to the Pensione Bencistà. I see the crowds and think how glad I am not to be waiting for the number 7 today—or perhaps I do wish I were heading up there, after reflecting on the benefits of solitude and retreat. I used to enjoy the windy journey as the bus made its way up the hill: seeing parts of the city that were beyond reasonable pedestrian limits, the transition from the city to the country, that first glimpse of the colourful Bencistà ensconced on the hillside.

The bus route continues the kilometre or so to Fiesole, which features a serene medieval Duomo; a complex with a Roman amphitheatre and a museum of Etruscan findings; and a block of restaurants shaded by a row of trees. A short but steep walk up to the top of another hill sits the convent of San Francesco, where the miniature rooms formerly inhabited by the Franciscans make

San Marco's cells seem palatial. It's hard to imagine living in such tight quarters, but they each have pretty views into the intimate cloistered herb garden or looking on to the countryside, and the convent's hilltop setting is very appealing.

From Piazza San Marco you can also see to the end of Via Cesare Battisti, all the way to the loggia in front of Santissima Annunziata. This church sits at the head of another piazza imprinted on my mind by my history of architecture professor. Piazza Santissima Annunziata was the first square to benefit from a consciously designed plan, instead of deriving from a mere widening in the road or whatever space could be opened up in front of the churches.

There was no outdoor public space to speak of when the Servites founded an oratory here in the mid-thirteenth century. Brunelleschi set the first element of order in place with his design for the Spedale degli Innocenti in 1419; the orphanage's most notable feature is the elegant loggia that runs along the front and became the unifying element of the piazza. The well proportioned arches of the arcade, which makes any misguided attempts at proportion appear especially dissonant—Piazza della Repubblica's arch comes to mind—guided the design of the piazza's other buildings. Symmetrical fountains and an equestrian statue of Grand Duke Ferdinando I completed the design two centuries later. The steps on opposite sides of the square make perfect seating for observing the markets and other events that fill this space throughout the year.

The church's particular fame stems from an episode that occurred soon after its founding. One of the friars was painting an

*Annunciation*, despairing that he could not do credit to the Madonna's loveliness. He fell asleep for a spell, and when he awoke he found that the painting had been completed: who but an angel could have been at work? Word of the miracle spread, and people travelled from all around to pray before the revered *Annunciation*, bringing hundreds of wax votive offerings; the cortile before the church was in fact built to house the continually expanding collection of wax figures, some of which were life-sized.

The celebration of the Madonna's birth on 8 September was Santissima Annunziata's most important day of all. The evening before, the families who lived in the country would begin their journey to the big mass and the market, holding lanterns to guide their way; this night-time trek brought about the tradition of the *Fiera della Rificolona* on 7 September. Just as Epiphany signifies the return to school after the Christmas holidays, the Rificolona is a sort of last fling before the school year starts the following week. The streets leading into the piazza are filled with children arriving from all around the city, carrying their colourful lanterns, which are still sometimes made by hand. There's a carnival atmosphere, with music, fairy floss, helium balloons and stands with bin after bin of sweets. 'Pea-shooters', traditionally the boys, make a sport of pelting the pretty lanterns with clay pellets, just as the city boys used to torment the country folk when they ventured into Florence.

I find myself near Piazza San Marco today, and thoughts of the delectable texture of Pugi's *schiacciata* draw me a little further north.

I can't resist trying the appealingly misshapen *Primavera* cake too—I taste chunks of apple, and maybe corn meal.

Pugi has a few seats at the back, but it's always more entertaining to find a bench in the piazza and watch the activity. Many of their customers appear to agree—the rubbish bins in the square are always overflowing with Pugi bags. The heat has sent most people to the shadier benches, although Piazza San Marco is not as shady as usual this summer; a harsh pruning has killed a couple of the trees and left the others struggling to leaf out to their typically generous fullness. The pigeons don't seem to mind the sun; they perch wherever there's space, some choosing a niche on the statue (which they have emphatically 'marked' as their territory), others preferring to parade around the square or just plop down unself-consciously in the middle of the pedestrian paths.

Watching all of the activity in Piazza San Marco, I think about how this piazza just goes about its business, day in, day out, with a noticeable break on Sundays, when commuters are few and Pugi is closed. Although important public events were held back when the Medici had ties with the square, I have never seen a parade or a market or concert in all the years I have been coming here. Season after season, the monochrome façade basks in the sun, just like the people who come seeking an oasis of tranquillity amid the chaos that surrounds the piazza.

# Piazzale Michelangelo

Visiting the area of Monte alle Croci to the south-east of Florence is one of my favourite rituals. And whether I go by bus, by car or on foot, the way up is as much a highlight as the view at the top. This escape beyond the confines of the city to the peaceful green hillside for a few hours equates taking a journey—perhaps not one of significant distance, but certainly of psychological proportions. I usually walk, if only for the pleasure of seeing where following the road will take my thoughts. Several pedestrian routes lead to the area's signature feature, Piazzale Michelangelo. You can wind slowly up the Viale dei Colli, take a meandering route along villa-lined Via San Leonardo, or ascend the formal Rampe di Poggi, which is named for the architect who designed the urban scheme for this area.

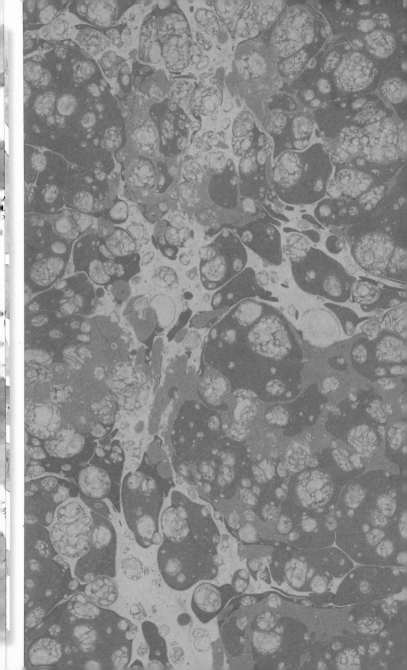

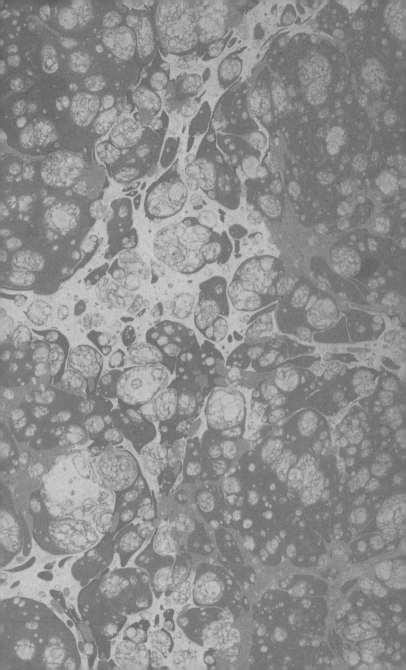

More often than not I choose the most direct way from my home, along Via de' Bardi. The street continues through Piazza Santa Maria Soprarno, where a modern bronze version of Saint John the Baptist looks as though it might be commanding traffic. I pass the shop where I like to buy my marbled-paper-covered journals, and then come to Palazzo Capponi delle Rovinate, so called because of the landslides that repeatedly used to damage the palace. A small arched opening and stone plaque remind passers-by that wine was once sold from the family's cantina. A wooden door, carved to mimic the stone wall that surrounds it, sits to its side. Walking down this street recently with a friend, I was fascinated by how her daughter discovered several more of these camouflaged doors by running her hands along the buildings, absorbing more information through her sense of touch than many of us do with our eyes.

A little further ahead is the church of Santa Lucia dei Magnoli, also nicknamed *delle Rovinate*, as it too was a victim of frequent landslides. Etched into a stone dated 1646, a notice states that games must be played one hundred *braccia*—about fifty-eight metres—away from the church. A similar rule of decorum still applies near the churches, although it doesn't tend to stop a nation of soccer lovers from kicking around any available ball. Nowadays, as motorcycles and cars race past, it's hard to imagine anyone playing on this narrow street. Opposite the church, a plaque on a retaining wall built to keep the landslides at bay notes Saint Francis's first visit to Florence in 1211, when he stayed at the pilgrim's hospice next to the church. The wall, with irises, ivy and wildflowers spontaneously sprouting from the top, concludes with a shrine-like display space—'the smallest art gallery in the world'—which often showcases cultural statements in the form of whimsical art.

As I follow the gently bending road, impressive *palazzi*, artisans' studios and workshops entertain my imagination. Curves decorate the worn stone window surrounds of some palaces; they are wonderfully tactile, of a quality that will never be produced again. We live in a different time, with more resources than ever, but not for details such as these.

In another *palazzo* is the lower entrance to the Parco Bardini, the same steep garden that can also be accessed at the top via the Boboli Garden. Part of the property belonged to the Mozzi family, who acquired land and constructed buildings and gardens in this area over a period of five centuries. After the family line died out, there were a couple of interim owners before antique- and art-collector Stefano Bardini purchased the vast property early in the twentieth century. Today the Bardini family name repeats and mingles with that of the Mozzi family at the intersection just beyond the garden: Palazzo Mozzi heads up a piazza of the same name, and Museo Mozzi-Bardini, a museum of eclectic pieces that Stefano assembled with the help of his son, sits on one corner.

I pass Palazzo Vegni, once the property of another old Florentine family. Behind the palace, the untamed Giardino Comunale climbs all the way up to the old city walls. I think of this garden as the Sunday Garden, since that's the only day it's open to the public. Just as well: by this time I usually feel overwhelmed by the many places where I would have liked to linger.

I walk through the cosy neighbourhood of San Niccolò, with its church, restaurants and shops, and then pass under Porta San Miniato, which signals the outer limit of the old medieval boundaries. Even before I reach the long flight of steps on Via San Salvatore al Monte, the jaunt up the hill has begun in earnest. At regular intervals, the simple crosses from a Stations of the Cross sequence mark my upward progress, and one hundred and sixty-two steps later I find myself, always breathless, next to a tempting display case of gelato.

First I go to the edge of Piazzale Michelangelo. A sea of terracotta rooftops separated by the Arno hovers below, presenting an intriguing overview of the city—as if one of those postcards of Florence has come to life.

Piazzale Michelangelo is listed in every guidebook and is on the itinerary of every tour bus for good reason: the lingering image of the city from here is unforgettable. This *piazzale*—'big piazza'—and the Viale dei Colli, a series of scenic roads winding up to it, were the happier results of a major urban plan implemented to celebrate Florence's interlude as Italy's capital. While on the plus side, citizens and visitors gained yet another way to enjoy the city, the loggia that was meant to house a museum dedicated to Michelangelo became instead the main feature of a restaurant, and the monument to the artist was reduced to a conglomeration of his most recognisable Florentine sculptures. The bronze figure of *David* rising among *Night*, *Day*, *Dusk* and *Dawn* sits right in the middle of a huge parking lot, among cars, tour buses and souvenir stands.

The most tragic note of the urban renewal project was that the final circuit of walls north of the river was demolished to allow room for another series of *viali*, the wide boulevards that still encircle Florence today. As with the 'revitalisation' of the Mercato Vecchio area that led to the addition of Piazza della Repubblica shortly afterwards, it's amazing the project gained approval. One wonders why architect Giuseppe Poggi preferred not to receive any particular recognition upon his death (his contributions to the city were many), but perhaps he felt a twinge of regret over his decision to remove Florence's walls?

While Poggi may not be buried among other famous individuals at Santa Croce, he is well remembered by the city. A piazza at Porta San Niccolò, and the *rampe* and *viale* that ascend from the riverfront piazza to Piazzale Michelangelo, all bear his name, and an enormous plaque at the piazza focuses not on the missing walls, but rather on his legacy of providing an eternal view over the city.

Despite the usual drawbacks of any popular tourist spot in Florence—crowds, footpaths covered with cheaply made reproductions of well known art, boxer shorts featuring *David*'s most talked about parts—I never tire of coming here. It's so satisfying to stand back and look at the city as a whole … appreciating the feeling of space, snapping new versions of Florence surrounded by so much sky (different every time), walking through wedding-celebration confetti that is part of the landscape, seeing the white satins and silks of brides billowing in the wind as they are photographed in the arms of their grooms.

A choice of shady parks in the area makes the visit to Piazzale Michelangelo even more enjoyable. On the first day of May, two additional gardens flanking the *piazzale* open to celebrate their blooms. Part way up that flight of one hundred and sixty-two steps is the Giardino delle Rose, whose several terraced levels set an intimate tone and present yet another perspective of the rooftops, bell towers and the ever-present curve of the cupola. It's a perfect spot for reading Anne Morrow Lindbergh's *Gift from the Sea* each spring. The sweet fragrance of lemon blossoms and dozens of roses often lulls me into lying on the grass, the book abandoned at my side for a while. The brief six weeks the garden stays open never seem long enough to take advantage of the many prime spots: next to a rose bush on the lower lawn; on a rock nestled in the Japanese Garden, which is tucked away in one corner; or under my favourite small olive tree on an upper terrace.

Irises are the focus of Giardino dell'Iris, which is found on the other side of Piazzale Michelangelo. The entrance is so obscure that it was some time before I knew it existed. Even once I read about it, my first casual looks didn't lead me to the gate, which only opens for the mere three weeks of May when the irises are (hoped to be) at their best.

The garden appears very much in a natural state, even a bit disorderly, with beds of irises seeming almost incidental to the scheme. I love its charming happenstance, the juxtaposition of the vehicles at the campsite on the other side of the fence. Lucky campers, sleeping in an olive grove with the garden next door (although I have heard there are plans to move the camping ground and create yet another garden).

It's fitting that Florence should be home to an iris garden: the so-called Florentine lily, or *giglio*, that has been the city's emblem since the founding of the *Comune* is really an iris. Growers from all over the world compete in the Concorso Internazionale dell'Iris, which has been held here every year since 1957. In addition to the more traditional prizes given, the *Premio Comune di Firenze* honours the iris whose colour comes closest to the clear red of the city's symbol. This is rather a challenge: while 'iris' derives from the Greek word for rainbow, and the flower does indeed exist in many colours, red is not one of its natural shades. As a result the entries are always variations on red—rusty-red, orangey-red, purpley-red.

The wildflowers and sweet roses, the fish in the pond at the bottom of the hill—and of course, the extraordinary irises—all combine to create a lovely backdrop for both private *pensieri* and shared confidences. Through repeat visits here, I have discovered that the beauty of irises goes considerably beyond the ubiquitous blue-purple ones that I have never really cared for. I have also learnt that it's worth saving conversation, energy, thoughts—and breath—

to make it back up to the top. On my first visit I was surprised to find that, after meandering down the steep site, the cruel reality is that you cannot then leave here, as logic might suggest. The walk back up, however, gives a fresh perspective on the garden, and certainly earns you a gelato.

Piazzale Michelangelo may offer an intimate look at the city, and a choice of *gelaterie* and cafés with a view, but the journey up here is not complete without a visit to the nearby church of San Miniato. From the terrace in front of the church is an even more expansive panorama of Florence and its surroundings, in an infinitely more peaceful setting.

There's the formal arrival planned by Poggi, where you stroll down the *viale* until reaching an impressive flight of steps; as you ascend, the church plays hide and seek behind the stairs, finally fully revealing itself at the top. I usually come the back way (the only way until Poggi revamped this area), continuing up the steps opposite those I take to reach Piazzale Michelangelo, passing the remaining Stations of the Cross that ends in front of the church of San Salvatore al Monte.

A little park sits on the last incline between San Salvatore and San Miniato. In the shade of umbrella pines and other evergreens, the older generation of Florentines set up lawn chairs brought from home, forming sociable conversational groups. Branches hover over one bench that sits on its own, creating a kind of outdoor room: Architecture designed by Nature. In this pleasant spot the late afternoon light is stunning and the shadows of trees move slowly

their modest shop. The sign on the apricot-coloured wall, garlanded with jasmine, reads: *Liquori e prodotti vari dei monaci Benedettini Olivetani*, 'Liqueurs and various products of the Olivetan Benedictine monks'. I look forward to looking through their flavoured honeys, natural health and beauty products, painted wooden trays and colourful ceramics, and always pick up a jar of *amarene* jam (made with sour cherries, and delicious on plain yoghurt, ice cream and pastries), as well as one of marmalade, the best I have ever tasted.

Along with the Baptistery of San Giovanni, San Miniato is a pure example of a Tuscan Romanesque church. The same style of contrasting marble patterns is seen on other existing traces of Romanesque churches around the city too—Santo Stefano, Santi Apostoli, San Salvatore al Vescovo. Their classically influenced designs foreshadowed the Renaissance architecture to come, and guided the other major Florentine church façades: Santa Maria Novella's fifteenth-century one, and those of the Duomo and Santa Croce in the nineteenth century.

The façade has so many details worth examining. And I always notice something new: how rain running down the bronze eagle at the highest point of the vault has caused the verdigris to run, tingeing even the white marble a shade of green; how a clump of lavender has somehow taken root and grows from the roof; how the same circular motifs from the interior repeat here, each with their own variations.

Taking a few extra minutes to study a building reminds me of one of my university professors, Harris Stone. The winter I finished his design studio, he suggested that it would be far more useful to sketch my experiences of an upcoming trip to Europe than it would be to merely write about them. I found he was right, and also discovered how difficult the most important key to drawing—simply taking time to look at a thing—can be, especially when travelling with others who are eagerly awaiting the next adventure.

I also think of Harris when I notice two small figures poking out at symmetrical points on the façade's lower pediment, their arms raised to 'carry' the weight above them, and then another pair of tiny men 'supporting' the roof of the central nave. Are they grimacing because of their eternal burdens? In *Diary of an Unsuccessful Architect*, Harris wrote about a 'person doubled-up, all but crushed by the weight he had to carry', which he had spotted under a plinth in the Strasbourg Cathedral. He observed that 'the mason who worked the stone knew just how dense it was. Through this figure he talked to me about his work and his life. I could comprehend the dead weight of the stone which he had shaped to appear light.' Now, whenever I notice signs of the individuals who built these timeless structures, I can't help but remember the delight Harris took in this little guy.

Stepping into the cool, dim basilica, one instantly grasps how a Romanesque church differs from a Gothic or Renaissance one, for although San Miniato's interior can be impressively bright at times, it was built when the structural know-how didn't yet allow for much natural light. Regardless, I always find the space inspiring. Instead of a volume sweeping continuously through the nave and all the way to the main altar, the rear third is broken up by a number of spaces that join on different levels: steps lead from the ground level up to the raised presbytery and also down into the crypt. A sense of harmony is created by the arch element from the façade, which repeats throughout the interior—along the side aisles, on the Cappella del Crocifisso in the nave, in the curve of the apse at the far end, in the diaphragm arches that separate the nave into three sections.

From the intricately patterned marble floor and the painted wooden roof trusses and ceiling, to the geometric marble and frescoed designs on the walls, the interior is beautifully detailed. I enjoy looking for the points where a motif changes, as if the worker had tired of the design and opted to move onto a new one. Or perhaps his son, continuing work in the following decade, decided it was time to reinvent the pattern. Somehow these frequent variations all work to form a harmonious, and much more interesting, whole.

The church of San Miniato is rich with legends. The story of the man who became known as San Minias fits in somewhere between the existence of an oratory dedicated to Saint Peter (where some of the first Christian martyrs took refuge) and the present eleventh-century structure. No one seems to know exactly who Minias was: he may have been the son of an Armenian king, a Roman soldier, or perhaps a Greek man. The difficulty in pinpointing the specifics of Florence's only martyr symbolises my quest to make sense of the city's entire history; fact merges with myth, and conflicting stories seem to turn up around every corner. While it can often be frustrating, I also appreciate the elusive quality—the fragility—of 'history', a word that traditionally carries such weight.

It is generally agreed that Minias was a Christian who was martyred during the reign of Emperor Decius, around 250 BC. Minias apparently carried his decapitated head up the hill to the same cave where he had retreated in life, and then died. An oratory dedicated to the saint's memory appeared at some point, but it wasn't until shortly after the first millennium that Bishop Ildebrando decided to replace the run-down building with a new basilica, which would be kept by the Benedictines.

Another legend centres on San Gualberto, the monk who founded the Vallombrosan order. Walking in these same hills on

Good Friday about a thousand years ago, Giovanni Gualberto met the man who had murdered his brother. The usual thing in those times would have been to take the murderer's life but, when the man begged for mercy, Giovanni pardoned him instead. Afterwards Giovanni went to pray before a crucifix in one of the many chapels that dotted the hillside in those days (some say it was actually at San Miniato), and the figure of Jesus apparently nodded its head in recognition of the act of forgiveness. This miracle inspired Giovanni to become a monk, and he joined the Benedictines in their convent at San Miniato. Ultimately, disgust over their corrupt ways caused him to leave. More than four hundred years later, a beautiful little chapel called the Cappello del Crocifisso was built to house the cross that had altered the course of the saint's life. While the chapel retains its original name, the crucifix has been moved to the Vallombrosan church of Santa Trìnita. It seems quite possible the transfer would have pleased San Gualberto.

A room-sized chapel honours the memory of Jacopo di Lusitania, a young Portuguese cardinal who died while passing through Florence in 1459. Three generations from what I think of as the 'family tree of artists'—a continually repeating cycle of masters and apprentices—were intrinsically part of this design of beautifully coordinated sculpture and painting within a classic space: Brunelleschi's Old Sacristy in San Lorenzo lent the inspiration for the chapel's form to his student, Antonio Manetti, and then Manetti's own student, Bernardo Rossellino, carved the cardinal's tomb and saw the project to its completion. The Pollaiolo brothers, Antonio and Piero, frescoed the wall behind their marble altarpiece (the original fresco is at the Uffizi), and medallions of the Holy Spirit and the Four Cardinal Virtues—which the young cardinal was said to have possessed—feature in a colourful ceramic ceiling by Luca della Robbia.

I am sitting on a stone ledge that extends from a wall near the Cappello del Crocifisso. From here I can see down into the crypt, where the monks began singing vespers as the bells chimed five. They sit along the edge of the apse, around the altar containing San Minias's relics, where traces of colourful frescoes brighten up the vaults overhead.

The monks create a lot of energy down in the crypt during this hour. Candles flicker, flowers grace the altar, and their uneven voices carry throughout the church. Part way through the mass, ignoring the confessional booths, one monk places a chair off to the side to hear confessions. This strikes me as incredibly lacking in privacy, although more discreet than the multilingual Plexiglass-walled confessional rooms in the side chapels at the Notre Dame in Paris.

I enjoy this chance to let my mind wander. It makes me think of Anne Morrow Lindbergh writing in *Gift from the Sea* about how the hour in church was traditionally the one time when women were guaranteed to be free of interruptions. I study the monks, who live so simply and seem to accept the process of aging so gracefully. A few are relatively young, but most are a bit hunched, balding and spectacled, and wear socks under their sensible sandals. What a contrast with the slick young Italian men, who drop in for mass wearing sporty leather lace-ups, tight jeans and chunky zippered sweaters, their masses of thick, dark wavy hair complemented by fashionable stubble.

Sometimes a perceptible sense of tension disrupts the tranquillity. When visitors enter the church they often aren't aware of the effect they have on the meditative atmosphere. Mobile phones occasionally ring, children run and cry out, and people can't seem to help but *chiacchierare*, chat—this is Italy, after all. Those seated in the pews may sometimes glare and click their tongues, but the monks are tolerant.

I look up at the capitals and lintels on the little *cappello;* each features a unique nature-inspired design carved in marble. What a shame they are too high up to touch. Through the open central doorway—a visual link from the church's interior to the city beyond—a row of cypress trees is silhouetted against the twilight sky. In the distance a plane descends towards Florence's airport; echoes from the sunset greet passengers returning home and offer a touch of magic for first-time visitors.

It's so dark in here now that it's hard to see the page before me, even with the spotlight from the chapel. Earlier, when I put a coin in the light machine for the main altar upstairs, the few tourists flocked around to see the huge mosaic illuminated, its gold tiles shimmering and the painted ceiling coming to life. The lights brought so much detail into view and utterly changed the quality of the space— illustrating the opposite of the adage 'out of sight, out of mind'.

Today I arrived with plenty of time to sit outside on the low wall that runs along the terrace, looking at the city nestled in the valley and enjoying the quarter-to-five bells joining those from all around the city. An Italian woman was sharing her knowledge of the church with a friend, and I watched them pick out landmarks in the cityscape. A few minutes later, on his way from the convent to vespers, one of the priests startled everyone by clapping an admonition to an amorous couple in the furthest corner.

It's wonderful to be able to see right into the city like this, wonderful how the cupola serves as a point of reference wherever one may be. And I appreciate how this chance to gaze down at the city is repeated on a smaller scale in the basilica itself: from the raised presbytery you can look into the nave, and from there into the crypt.

221

Being able to observe the space from different perspectives makes it possible to experience the church of San Miniato more fully than a church where you only have a limited vantage point.

Adjacent to the main altar on the upper level is the sacristy, a room featuring a single enormous cross vault. A mottled blue ceiling sprinkled with gold stars crowns a series of sixteen three-dimensional-looking frescoes illustrating the legend of Saint Benedict, known for the Rule he wrote to counsel fellow monks on their religious paths. I lean against the radiator to absorb its faint warmth and notice an eagle suspended from the centre of the ceiling. This is the symbol of the *Arte di Calimala*, the guild of the refiners of imported wool, who funded the church. The eagle would make a great theme for a treasure hunt. There are so many, and in a number of different materials and media: frescoed on walls and ceilings, carved from marble and wood into bas-reliefs and statuettes, cast into bronze figures …

From tiny windows in a set of doors near the sacristy you can see the cloister tucked into the monks' living quarters. It is characterised by rather squat proportions and substantial square columns—most unlike the elegant Renaissance loggias that run around many of Florence's urban cloisters, but still possessing the same appealing sense of rhythm and play of light and shadow. The cloister was rebuilt in about 1426, and although they aren't visible through the windows, frescoes by Paolo Uccello from that period were discovered under layers of whitewash in the twentieth century. According to Vasari, Uccello—a dedicated master of perspective—was fed not much more than cheese as he worked on these frescoes; too timid to protest, he ran away mid-project. Apparently, when a pair of monks from San Miniato discovered the reason for his disappearance and reported back to the abbot, he promised there would be no more cheese, and Uccello finally finished the frescoes.

The cloister is surrounded by the crenellated building to the right of the church, which was designed as the bishop's summer palace at the same time that work began on the Duomo. After just a few decades, the palace was absorbed into the convent and went on to serve several other functions over the centuries: as a barracks in the sixteenth century, a hospital the following century, and then a hospice. In 1924 the Olivetan Benedictines assumed responsibility for the complex, and they still take care of the monastery here.

I was about to head for home when a few startling notes from the organ broke the solemnity that fills the basilica after vespers. I am not usually drawn to organ music, but the monk who sometimes plays here does so with an engaging enthusiasm that makes it hard to leave. The music is a dramatic accompaniment as I look over the pavement of Zodiac symbols and animals, which reminds me of an oriental carpet, and watch the monks socialising with the congregation after closing up the crypt for the night.

San Miniato preserves such a lovely relationship with the past, staying forever connected to the city by the iconic façade that is visible even from down in the centre. It has worn so beautifully through the centuries. The church may remain the same, and mass continue to be celebrated here each day, but according to the hour, the day of the week and the religious calendar, my experience here is always different. The basilica can be full of light in summer, or eerie and dank on a short winter day; it cools my skin when I come in from the July sun and chills me to the bone in January. An international mix of visitors often outnumbers the regular locals—or sometimes neither is present. One winter afternoon a storm had caused dark to fall unusually early, and I was the only outsider attending vespers. It felt almost surreal sitting in the freezing cold shadows of the vast space, so silent without the usual commotion of a constant flux of visitors, the monks' singing becoming part of the setting:

Coming back outside, I am reminded of Michelangelo's contribution up at San Miniato. During the Siege of 1529–30, when Charles V besieged Florence in an attempt to get on the good side of Medici Pope Clement VII, the city leaders asked Michelangelo to build fortifications encircling the area around San Miniato. Two cannons were placed in the campanile, a half-built replacement for one that had collapsed. The bell tower itself therefore became a target, but legend says that by screening it with woollen mattresses and cotton bales, Michelangelo was able to prevent its destruction; today you can still see traces of fire and bullets on one side of the tower, which has remained unfinished after all these years. While the bell tower survived, the Republic fared less well—after ten months the Medici returned to power.

You can get a full view of the bell tower from the cemetery behind the church. The boundaries of the Cimitero Monumentale delle Porte Sante, built in the second half of the nineteenth century, follow the outline of the old fortifications. Walking among the simple slabs, funerary sculpture and elaborate marble 'houses' of the wealthy, it's hard not to contemplate what will become of one's own remains upon death.

The best time to walk through the cemetery is on the first day of November, All Saints' Day. This will be the most life that fills the space all year, as families honour their loved ones with visits and flowers. It feels somewhat intrusive to witness the grief of strangers, but it's important to have reminders of the living against what W.D. Howells called 'a place to make one laugh and cry with the hideous vulgarity of its realistic busts and its photographs set in the tombstones; and yet it is one of the least offensive in Italy.

When I could escape from the fascination of its ugliness, I went and leaned with my friend on the parapet that encloses the Piazza Michelangelo, and took my fill of delight in the landscape.'

As I, too, return to Piazzale Michelangelo, the distinctive bells of San Miniato mark the hour. Standing at the stone balustrade that surrounds the piazza, I think about how a visit here—or to the other hillside viewing spots—seems to satisfy a psychological need to see the horizon, which isn't often visible from within the city.

I also come up for the chance to observe the city as a whole. I love the charm of hill towns, but they can appear unapproachable, imposing, remote, as they look down on you. And while a hilltop may offer a valuable strategic position, you can't really read these high-up towns as you can a river town like Florence, where vantage points among the surrounding hills and at the top of the cathedral make it so easy to grasp the basic relationships between Florence's landmarks.

I am often inclined to define why I feel so much at home in Florence when this view is before me. Part of the reason may be that which prompted author R.W.B. Lewis to call Florence a 'knowable city'. He wrote: 'A real city—that is a knowable city—does good things for one's identity; in knowable surroundings, one arrives at a firmer grasp of the self.' Every Italian town I have visited so far seems to possess a quintessential quality—layers of detail wrought from a long history. But Florence continues to be the one that intrigues me most. Elegant in its simplicity, the city remains rational, explainable, yet under its logical appearance lies an element of surprise, of mystery.

Even more important is the everyday appeal of walking around Florence, living with the daily rhythms of the fabric that holds it together. I find the pedestrian scale to be remarkably synergistic, that it impacts our quality of life in such a positive way. The level of human contact helps us feel connected with the city and its people; as a consequence we are tied to our neighbourhood in a way we have never been anywhere else. I subconsciously ignore the sometimes annoyingly narrow footpaths, the dogs relieving themselves on those footpaths (surprisingly, I have yet to misstep), cigarette butts everywhere, graffiti on the walls.

After months of frequenting the same café every day, I am finally getting to know the other regulars. It has taken time to get acquainted with the neighbours too, but after numerous encounters on the steps, we received our first invitation to dinner. A little at a time, it feels as if we are finding a place among the people who make up our city. The slow pace suits me though; it allows people to develop a context—like reading a novel the old-fashioned way, in instalments. I never have been one for page-turners.

Sometimes I ask myself why I, who so enjoy solitude, have chosen to live in this most sociable of countries, in the middle of a city, with its commotion and confusion. But Florence itself draws me into participating, and this wish to be part of all it offers doesn't show any sign of disappearing. I still feel the same excitement I experience in a city that's new to me, or upon returning to a favourite like Paris or Hong Kong. Occasional absences over the past few years have only strengthened my feeling that Florence is indeed where I feel most at home.

As I walk down those one hundred and sixty-two steps and pass through Porta San Miniato, the sounds of the city become noticeable once again: the return to chaos. My brain switches modes. I always enjoy the short break, but instantly remember why I prefer the centre—all those diverging angles of the terracotta rooflines, the striking light and shadow on the stone of the medieval towers and Renaissance *palazzi*, the delicate contrasting marble patterns decorating many of the church façades, and the honest bareness of others, the verticality of the cypress trees serving as occasional exclamation marks. And even though Florence may be a 'knowable' city, as I wander through the streets, pause in the piazzas, relax in the gardens and parks, I have no doubt that a new discovery is waiting—that there will be another Italian mystery to solve … or not.

# Acknowledgments

I have witnessed a tremendous amount of enthusiasm, energy and assistance while writing this book. So many people have contributed, from our many visiting friends and family—who always give me the chance to see the city through fresh eyes—to the locals who make our everyday lives in Florence such a pleasure.

In particular, I'd like to thank my family for their encouragement and endless offers of help: they are a creative group of individuals, and their unique approaches and strengths have each benefited this book as it has taken shape. My parents, Dick and Sue, made the role of ex-pat seem so natural that I thought nothing of taking it on myself—thank you for giving us a childhood rich with travel, and for continuing the tradition of introducing me to new places even now. My sister Kelly is always ready for a brainstorming session—thank you for your willingness to endlessly discuss 'the book' (and I don't know what I would have done without you last summer). It's good to know that my brother, Mark, and my sister-in-law, Aimée, are always 'there'—thank you for your constant support. And a huge thank you to my daughter—dear Ella, you have been amazing in countless ways, and you are such an inspiration.

I thank Andy McGarry for his continued enthusiasm for my writing projects, and for talking about the book (in its various forms over the years) to everyone he meets. I am grateful to my generous and patient friends for still being my friends even when I said no to lunch or coffee too often. A special thank you to Tessa Kiros—for the inspiration you have been as an individual, a friend and an author. I would also like to acknowledge the many other authors and artists whose work has motivated me during this journey—my bookshelves are rich with the words of your wisdom and experiences.

Without Kay Scarlett at Murdoch, this book would never have become all that it is—thank you for your vision, your faith and your trust. A big thank you to the dedicated team who saw the book to its completion: Emma Hutchinson—for your deft organisation of every aspect of the project, including your many valuable insights; Sarah Baker and Colette Vella—for your attentive assistance with the manuscript; and Reuben Crossman—for the design that so beautifully holds it all together.

Closer to home, I'd like to say *grazie mille* to Marco and Cinzia, the owners of the café in the tiny piazza that has become a part of my daily life—thank you for the perfect second 'office', for the delicious morning coffee, for expanding my musical horizons.

And I will always be grateful to the many Florentines who have made me feel so at home here—including those I will never meet, but who played a part in shaping Florence so long ago …

# *Reading list*

**Travel narratives.** *I particularly enjoy seeing how Florence has changed over time, and yet how much has remained the same. It's also interesting to read the later authors' comments on the earlier books.*

Merrill Joan Gerber, *Botticelli Blue Skies*, The University of Wisconsin Press, Madison, Wisconsin, 2002. Unlike the typically enthusiastic visitor to Italy, Gerber begins an autumn sojourn in Florence rather reluctantly. Once she gets settled, however, she finds a happy rhythm and ends up making several enjoyable discoveries.

W.D. Howells, *Tuscan Cities*, Ticknor & Co, Boston, 1886. This book opens with 'A Florentine Mosaic', in which Howells relates his experiences and observations while visiting Florence's many attractions.

Henry James, *Italian Hours*, Houghton Mifflin Co., Boston, 1909. This collection of essays, written during James's many stays in a number of cities in Italy, includes many reflections on Florence.

R.W.B. Lewis, *The City of Florence, Historical Vistas and Personal Sightings*, Farrar, Straus and Giroux, New York, 1995. I have enjoyed reading this book many times since I picked it up on my first trip to Florence in 1996. Lewis outlines Florence's history before delving deeper into several of Florence's neighbourhoods as he shares his experiences of living in each.

E.V. Lucas, *A Wanderer in Florence*, The Macmillan Company, New York, 1912. This entertaining and congenial portrayal of the city is filled with history, legends and anecdotes.

Mary McCarthy, *The Stones of Florence*, Harcourt Brace Javonovich, New York, 1959. A sharp and well informed classic narrative about Florence, this large-format edition is illustrated with striking full-page photographs.

H.V. Morton, *A Traveller in Italy*, Dodd, Mead & Company, New York, 1964. This prolific and well travelled writer devotes a long chapter to Florence and its many interesting stories.

John Ruskin, *Mornings in Florence*, Donohue, Henneberry & Co., Chicago (first published 1875). Originally published as a collection of booklets to accompany visitors as they spent mornings exploring Florence, it has become a classic. Possibly one of the most frequently quoted books about Florence, the author's critical assessment of Florence's monuments and art has sparked reactions ranging from appreciative to amused to indignant.

**Guides and Histories.** *A brief list of favourites.*

Eve Borsook, *The Companion Guide to Florence*, Companion Guides, Woodbridge, UK, 2000, reprint of sixth revised edition (first published 1966). More than a thorough guide to Florence and its churches, palaces and gardens. I particularly enjoy reading the focus essays for each chapter; in a more personal approach, Borsook explores Florence's culture, politics and key families in more depth while giving a flavour for the Florence she knows.

Helen Gardner, Horst de la Croix and Richard G. Tansey, *Art Through the Ages*, Harcourt Brace Javonovich, New York, 1986, eighth edition (first published 1926). One of the texts used for the series of architectural history courses I took at university, this one remains a favourite. Each chapter is introduced with a map and a timeline focusing on the period it explores, and there are sections on painting, sculpture and architecture from ancient times to the present. Italy appears in several chapters.

Christopher Hibbert, *Biography of a City*, The Folio Society, London, 1997 (first published 1993). A beautiful edition of a very knowledgeable history, engagingly told, featuring a 'guide' to Florence's major monuments at the end.

Alta Macadam, *City Guide: Florence* (Blue Guide), A&C Black, London, 2001, eighth edition. Compact and detailed, this is a very useful guidebook with good floor plans and sketches of Florence's major attractions.

Giorgio Vasari, abridged and edited by Betty Burroughs, *Lives of the Artists*, Simon & Schuster, New York, 1946. Many of the anecdotes about the multi-talented artists that we find in more contemporary narratives and histories rely on the accounts by Vasari. His entertaining *Lives* brings each of these individuals to life.

## Books by Florentines

Piero Bargellini (English translation by Brenda Nicholls and Robert McPierce), *Florence the Magnificent: A History*, Vallecchi Editore, Firenze, 1980, second edition. A four-volume, extensively illustrated work written by one of Florence's former mayors, who shares the colourful stories that make up his beloved city's history.

Cristina Degl'Innocenti and Chiara Bartolini (with English text by Robin Poppelsdorff), *Diladdarno*, Edizioni Polistampa, Firenze, 2003. Focusing on the area to the south side of the river, this book of beautiful photographs is accompanied by a sensitive and rich text in Italian and English, which weaves the area's history into its present.

Giovanni Fanelli, *La Vita Urbana nel Corso del Tempo*, APT (Agenzia per Turismo), Firenze, 2003. A collection of six booklets focuses on the changes in Florence's major piazzas and streets over the centuries, and includes diagrams, drawings, paintings and photographs. Fanelli, a local architecture professor, has written several books about Florence, and his material has been extracted for several APT publications.

Mario Mariotti, *Piazza S. Spirito*, Edizioni Alinari, Firenze, 1981. This book documents Mariotti's façade project for the church of Santo Spirito, and includes essays and photos of the festivities as well as drawings and projections for the façade designs.

For a first-hand account of climbing up into Andrea Verrocchio's ball at the top of the cupola, go to: http://www.vps.it/new_vps/articolo_eng.php?article=12

**Fiction set in Florence.** *Each of these novels is set in Florence (or, in the case of* Portrait of a Lady, *partially so), and engagingly portrays a particular historical period.*

George Eliot, *Romola*, Thomas Y. Crowell & Co., New York (first serialised in 1862–63). Set in the late fifteenth century, upon the death of Lorenzo il Magnifico and when Savonarola was beginning to take control of Florence. This is the epic story of Romola, an intelligent but naive young woman who faces the consequences of her poor choice of husband.

Robert Hellenga, *The Sixteen Pleasures*, Soho Press, New York, 1994. Margot Harrington stumbles onto an unexpected discovery while using her book-restoration expertise to help out at a local convent after Florence's devastating 1966 flood.

W. D. Howells, *Indian Summer*, Houghton Mifflin Company, The Riverside Press, Cambridge, Boston, 1885. Theodore Colville is an American man confronting his romantic feelings towards a younger woman in this novel that conveys the flavour of late nineteenth-century Florence.

Henry James, *Portrait of a Lady*, Houghton, Mifflin and Company, Boston, 1881. The woman in question is an independent young American, Isabel Archer, who struggles with the choices she makes once her world opens up on a visit to Europe.

Magdalen Nabb, *Death of an Englishman*, Collins, London, 1981. This is the first of a series of mysteries by Nabb that are set in my neighbourhood. Nabb lived in Florence for thirty-seven years, and her mysteries, featuring the likeable Marshal Guarnaccia, convey a vivid sense of character and place.

**Books that inspire.** *A handful of books that I turn to often.*

Christopher Alexander, *A Pattern Language*, Center for Environmental Structure, Berkeley, California, 1975. This second book of a three-volume series explores the nuts and bolts of creating a more livable, more human environment through a series of two hundred and fifty-three patterns.

Akiko Busch, *Geography of Home*, Princeton Architectural Press, New York, 1999. Beginning with the front door, the author takes readers through the typical rooms of a house, exploring the original use of each room and the way in which their function—and indeed the need for each—has changed over time.

Alain de Botton, *The Art of Travel*, Pantheon Books, New York, 2002. De Botton meditates on many aspects of travel, from why we do so to how we might improve our journeys. Each chapter's theme features a 'place', from Madrid to Barbados to The Lake District, and a 'guide', from Gustave Flaubert to John Ruskin to Vincent van Gogh.

Anne Morrow Lindbergh, *Gift from the Sea*, Pantheon Books, New York, 1992 (first published 1955). This beautifully written book of essays about accepting the joys and challenges of the different stages of a woman's life serves as a gentle reminder to honour each phase.

Marlene McLouglin, *Road to Rome*, Chronicle Books, San Francisco, 1995. The artist uses a gorgeous palette of watercolours to depict her journey from Florence to Rome.

Sara Midda, *South of France Sketchbook*, Workman, New York, 1990. This is a favourite book: to hold, to browse, to linger with. The artist transforms the French flag in a dozen unexpected fresh images, portrays her search for the perfect birthday gift for a friend into a clever series of illustrations, gives life to pastries, olives and other French delicacies with her distinctive watercolours.

Doug Lew, *Watercolor Journal of Florence*, Mandragora, Florence, 2002. An evocative visual record of the author's visit, this series of on-site watercolours, each accompanied by the artist's comments, offers inspiration and advice on techniques.

# Glossary

**Aisle** The areas that run along both sides of a church's nave, separated by columns and distinguished by a lower ceiling.

**Campanile** The Duomo's freestanding bell tower, also called the Campanile di Giotto, after its original architect.

**Counter façade** The interior façade of a building.

**Counter-reformation** A late-sixteenth-century reform instigated when the Catholic Church was in the middle of a campaign to prevent its members from becoming Protestants.

**Crossing** The area that lies at the intersection of the nave and the transepts.

**Crypt** The lower level of a church, used as a chapel and/or burial place.

**Drum** The walls that support a dome.

**Duomo** Literally 'house of God', this is what the Italians call their cathedrals. Cattedrale di Santa Maria del Fiore is the official name of Florence's Duomo.

**Fresco cycle** Created using a technique of painting onto fresh plaster, fresco cycles feature a series of scenes portraying stories from the Bible.

**Ghibellines** The pro-emperor faction in medieval times, they alternately shared power with the Guelphs.

**Guelphs** The pro-papacy faction, after definitively defeating the Ghibellines in 1266, further divided into the Neri, the more extreme members, and the Bianchi, the more moderate branch. When the Bianchi were exiled in 1302, Dante was among them. He never returned to Florence.

**House of Lorraine** In 1737, upon the death of the last male Medici, Gian Gastone, the Austrian Lorraine family assumed the title of grand duke, ruling with few interruptions until Tuscany joined the newly united Italy in 1865.

**House of Savoy** The Savoy family ruled the Republic of Italy from 1860; they took up residence at Palazzo Pitti when the capital was transferred to Florence between 1865 and 1871.

**Lantern** A windowed structure at the top of a dome that allows light in.

**Loggia** An open covered space. A large public loggia, the Loggia dei Lanzi, was built in Piazza della Signoria, but many of the private *palazzi* also featured loggias.

**Medici** A wealthy banking family intrinsically linked with Florence's history, the Medici ruled Florence for the better part of three centuries. As patrons of the arts, they made vast contributions to the shape of the city through the buildings and art they commissioned.

**Mendicant order** A number of religious orders began settling in Florence in the early- to mid-thirteenth century, including the Dominicans, the Franciscans, the Augustinians, the Servites and the Carmelites. Unlike the traditional cloistered monks, these friars did not own any property and so had to depend on alms for their support. Their intent was to involve the laity.

**Nave** The main portion of the church, where the congregation sits.

**Piazza** (also *piazzale*, big piazza; *piazzetta*, little piazza) Florence's streets open onto dozens of these public outdoor spaces, which can range from a tiny widening of the road to a square large enough to host sporting events, concerts and city-wide celebrations.

**Sacristy** A separate room where the sacred vestments are stored and where the priest prepares for the mass.

**Stations of the Cross** A work consisting of fourteen representations of the incidents leading up to Jesus's crucifixion, it can be as simple as a series of numbered crosses or take the form of more elaborate and detailed bas-reliefs or sculptures in stone, wood or metal.

**Transept** The two arms that project at right angles from a church's nave.

**Vasari Corridor** The overhead passage built by the Medici family for their safe and convenient passage from their home in Palazzo Pitti to their offices at the Uffizi.

## Terms in Italian

*Alimentari* (small grocery store) These shops stock basic food staples and feature a case of deli meats, cheese, olives, etc.

*Aperitivo* (cocktail) Cocktail hour is generally between 7 and 9 in the evening. Bars typically set out little plates of snacks to accompany wine, prosecco or mixed drinks.

*Arte*, pl. *arti* (guild) Florence had seven major and five minor guilds; their members regulated trade and were eligible for the drawing of the new members of the *Signoria* every two months. This group consisted of eight *Priori* and one *Gonfaloniere*, who bore the honour of bearing the city's banner.

*Baldacchino* (baldachin) A canopied structure over an altar.

*Battistero* (baptistery) This designated place for the ceremony of baptism was traditionally often a separate building, as is Florence's, called the Battistero di San Giovanni.

*Belle arti* A shop selling art supplies.

*Caffè* In a general sense this means café (although a café is often called a 'bar' here), but it's also the name used for the strong shot of coffee that non-Italians typically call an espresso. A *caffè macchiato* is 'stained' with milk, and a *caffè latte* has more milk and less foam than a cappuccino. The Italians seem to be catching on to the fact that when the foreigners ask for a *latte* (which means 'milk' in Italian), they often want a *caffè latte*, so will often check before presenting a cup of milk.

*Cartoleria* (stationery shop) These sell everything from school and office supplies to basic craft materials and toys.

*Calcio in costume* An event consisting of a series of three games played between the four quarters of the city each summer. The sport is based on a traditional game that combines soccer, rugby and wrestling and the players dress in historic costume.

*Carnevale* (carnival) This period of celebration before Lent begins after the Christmas holidays; there are special treats at the bakery, children (and adults) dress in costume and litter the streets and piazzas with *corriandolo* (colourful bits of paper) and a parade takes place the Sunday before Lent begins.

*Cenacolo* (refectory) This room in a convent was traditionally decorated with a depiction of the Last Supper. Several of these *Last Suppers* remain in the original context of the *cenacoli* and are open to the public.

*Centro* The area of Florence that lies within the final set of walls, which UNESCO designated as a World Heritage Site; also known as the *centro storico*, historic centre. The Oltrarno, literally 'beyond the Arno', is more specifically the area of Florence to the south side of the river, and is also known as Diladdarno.

*Chiostro* (cloister) This open space lies at the heart of a convent or monastery and typically features a garden surrounded by arcaded walks.

*Cioccolata* (hot chocolate) The Florentine version is thick and not very sweet, and is often offered with *panna*, cream.

*Comune* Florence began organising itself into a municipality back in the early thirteenth century, called the *Comune*. The *Comune* can refer to members of the local government or Palazzo Vecchio, where their offices are housed.

*Corteo Storico della Repubblica Fiorentina and Bandierai degli Uffizi* The Corteo Storico consists of five hundred Florentines dressed in historic costume; they parade through the city for a number of events through the year. They are often accompanied by the Bandierai, or flag throwers, who show off their flag-throwing skills.

*Cotto* (literally, 'cooked') This can refer to the terracotta ('cooked earth') tiles traditionally used for floors, and also on ceilings in conjunction with wooden beams. The term is also used for food, such as *prosciutto cotto*, cooked ham.

*Ex convento* (ex-convent) In the early nineteenth century convents all over Europe were suppressed and the property of the religious entities taken over by the State. Florence's ex-convents now serve a number of purposes, including military and artistic spaces.

*Latteria* A small shop selling dairy products, and often associated with a bar or *alimentari*.

*Lungarno*, pl. *lungarni* The streets that run along the Arno river are several metres higher than the riverbanks; each stretch has its own name.

*Mesticheria* A shop selling basic items for the home.

*Palazzo*, pl. *palazzi*; *palazzina* and *palazzetto* are both diminutive forms (palace). *Palazzo* can also refer to any multi-storey building in the city. Palazzo del Popolo, built in 1252 and now called the Bargello, was the first civic palace. Palazzo Vecchio, which replaced it at the turn of the thirteenth century, has served as the city hall for over seven centuries. Florence still features dozens of Renaissance *palazzi*, which were built by the wealthy citizens.

*Pietre dure*, hard semi-precious stone, available in a multitude of colours and used to create intricate patterns and designs. The Museo dell'Opificio delle Pietre Dure displays a collection of work executed in *pietre dure*.

*Pietra forte* A very hard, warm-coloured stone used to build many of Florence's public and private *palazzi*.

*Pietra serena* Much softer than *pietra forte*, this greyish stone is used for interior details and makes a striking contrast against the white plaster walls.

*Primo* (first) This word often refers to the first course of a meal, which typically consists of soup, pasta or risotto.

*Quartiere* (quarter, or neighbourhood) Florence has four quarters: San Giovanni, Santa Maria Novella, Santa Croce and Santo Spirito.

*Sciopero* (strike) Strikes—for everything from transportation to schools to government offices—are part of daily life in Italy.

*Tabacchi* Traditionally a tobacco shop; they also recharge mobile phones, sell bus tickets, stamps, lottery tickets, sweets, postcards and more.

*Viale*, pl. *viali* (boulevard) Florence is ringed by a series of boulevards, which follow the perimeter of the final set of city walls (demolished in the late nineteenth century).

First published in 2008 by Pier 9, an imprint of Murdoch Books Pty Limited

Murdoch Books Australia
Pier 8/9
23 Hickson Road
Millers Point NSW 2000
Phone: +61 (0)2 8220 2000
Fax: +61 (0)2 8220 2558
www.murdochbooks.com.au

Murdoch Books UK Limited
Erico House, 6th Floor
93–99 Upper Richmond Road
Putney, London SW15 2TG
Phone: +44 (0) 20 8785 5995
Fax: +44 (0) 20 8785 5985
www.murdochbooks.co.uk

Chief Executive: Juliet Rogers
Publishing Director: Kay Scarlett
Project Manager: Emma Hutchinson
Editor: Sarah Baker
Design concept: Reuben Crossman
Design layout: Reuben Crossman and Hugh Ford
Production: Nikla Martin
Text and artwork copyright © Lisa McGarry 2008
Design copyright © Murdoch Books Pty Limited 2008

National Library of Australia Cataloguing-in-Publication Data:
McGarry, Lisa.
The piazzas of Florence
Includes bibliography.
ISBN 978 1 7419 6089 1 (hbk.)
Piazzas–Italy--Florence. Architecture–Italy–Florence.
Florence (Italy)–Buildings, structures, etc. Florence
(Italy)–Description and travel. Florence (Italy)–History.
711.55094551

A catalogue record for this book is available from the British Library.

across the wall of the Franciscan Missionary Centre next to San Salvatore. I have tried to record the effect in a small study in oils, but really a whole series would be needed to explore the ever-changing shadows, the way the foliage captures the sun as the hours pass, the sense of structure created by the tree trunks.

Parco della Rimembranza, a swathe of land where rows of cypresses have grown tall, lies just outside the ramparts that surround the complex of San Miniato. They march proudly up the hillside, calling to mind the volunteer nurses and military personnel that the Red Cross honours with this memorial.

In his book *A Wanderer in Florence*, E.V. Lucas wrote '... when all is said the S. Miniato habit is the most important to acquire', referring to his belief that repeat visits to Florence's churches only increase one's enjoyment of them. I agree, and also feel that San Miniato, which offers a glimpse far back into Florence's history of distinctive churches, stands out from the others. It's not just the setting, up on a hill surrounded by grassy areas with wildflowers and birds singing, but also the air of serenity that permeates the area.

While the church of San Miniato has the usual outdoor space before it, the feeling is very different from that of a typical urban piazza with sociable cafés, shops, fountains and museums. I find it the most receptive of the churches, perhaps because the terrace so generously presents one of the most spectacular views over the city. But the monks who care for the church and live in the monastery next door also add to the impression of welcome: there is a standing invitation to join them for vespers each afternoon and to browse in

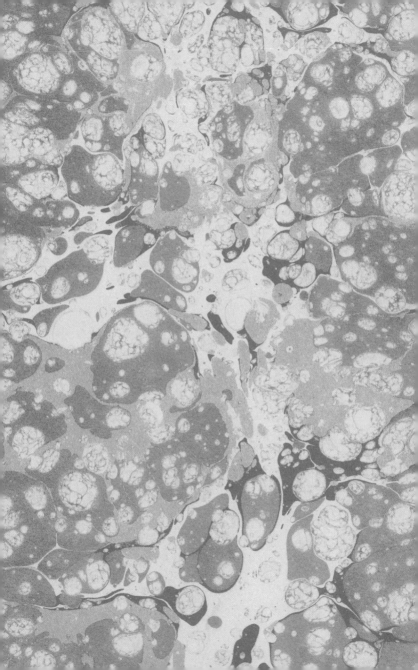

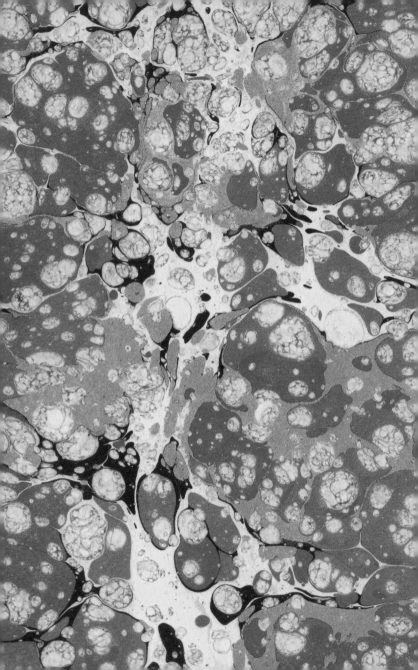